Mastering Time for Productivity

A Guide to Improve Efficiency in Work and Life

Ellen Sedge

Impisi Media LLC

ISBN: 978-1-965722-00-8 (eBook)
ISBN: 978-1-965722-01-5 (Paperback)
ISBN: 978-1-965722-16-9 (Hardcover)

The case studies in this book are based on real-life experiences. To protect privacy, names, locations, and identifying details have been changed or omitted. Any resemblance to persons, businesses, or places beyond the intended examples is coincidental. The lessons and insights are genuine and provide practical guidance to readers on their entrepreneurial journey.

Book design by Ciska Venter.

First printing edition 2024.

Published by Impisi^{TM} Media LLC in the United States of America.
5830 E 2ND ST, STE 7000, CASPER, WY 82609, +1 (307) 275 8745
www.impisimedia.com
Impisi^{TM} is subject to a trademark application by Impisi Media LLC.

Contents

Also by the Publisher

Small Business Series

Should You Start a Business or Not?
Business Entry: Starting vs Buying
3 Keys to Maximize Profitability

Smart Work-Life Series

Mastering Time for Productivity
The Wolf's Edge – Strategies for Intelligent Living
Reset with Intermittent Fasting

Click or scan the QR code to receive updates on new releases and book resources.

"Everything should be made as simple as possible, but not simpler."

Albert Einstein

Introduction

"The bad news is time flies. The good news is you're the pilot."

Michael Altshuler

Purpose of the Book

Time is one of the most valuable assets in entrepreneurship. Managing it effectively often determines the difference between success and failure. This book helps entrepreneurs harness the power of time management to drive productivity, leading to increased profitability. Whether you're already in business or just starting, the strategies and insights here will offer valuable guidance.

Time management goes beyond being just a buzzword; it's a critical skill influencing every business aspect. From setting priorities to improving daily operations, how you manage your time will determine how efficiently your business runs.

This book explores practical techniques and tools to help you master this essential skill. You'll become more productive and build a more profitable and sustainable business by improving your time management.

But productivity isn't just about working harder—it's about getting smarter to get things done. This book emphasizes balancing, putting in the necessary effort, and enjoying your work. Many entrepreneurs fall into the trap of working endlessly, believing that more hours automatically lead to better results. However, this approach leads to burnout and diminished returns without proper time management. This book aims to guide you in striking the right balance, ensuring that your hard work translates into meaningful outcomes.

One key goal of this book is to help you manage your business in a way that supports both your professional and personal life. As an entrepreneur, it's easy to get caught up in the demands of your business, often at the expense of your well-being. This book offers strategies to help you achieve financial success and a fulfilling and enjoyable entrepreneurial journey.

In conclusion, this book equips you with the tools and knowledge to manage your time effectively, boost your productivity, and ultimately improve your business's profitability. By focusing on these core areas, you will be better positioned to thrive in the competitive world of small business while keeping a healthy work-life balance.

How to Use This Book

Time management involves organizing and allocating your time effectively to achieve your goals. It requires making conscious decisions on how you spend each hour, setting clear priorities, and using proven strategies to maximize your limited time.

This book guides you through mastering these principles with practical advice and actionable steps.

In this guide, you'll explore various topics related to productivity and time management, including:

- **Time Tracking and Analysis**: Understand how to track your time and analyze your patterns, so you can identify areas for improvement and increase your efficiency.

- **Effective Goal Setting and Prioritization**: Learn to set clear, achievable goals that motivate and inspire action, and prioritize tasks that will have the greatest impact on your success.

- **Task Management Systems**: Explore tools and methods for organizing and managing tasks, from simple to-do lists to advanced project management software.

- **Mastering Productivity with Time Blocking**: Organize your day into dedicated blocks for specific tasks or activities, enhancing your focus and productivity.

- **Mastering Focus and Concentration**: Develop techniques to maintain deep focus and concentration, enabling you to work more effectively and do more in less time.

- **Energy Management in Productivity**: Implement strategies for managing your energy levels throughout the day, ensuring you stay productive and avoid burnout.

- **Stress Management**: Learn techniques to manage stress and maintain balance, even during busy times, so you can stay focused and effective.

- **Conquering Procrastination**: Develop methods to overcome procrastination, maintain motivation, and consistently move towards your goals.

Whether you aim to increase productivity at work, streamline daily routines, or find more time for what matters most, this book provides the knowledge, tools, and inspiration needed to take control of your time and reach your full potential.

To get the most out of this book, consider reading it from start to finish, as each chapter builds on the earlier one. Alternatively, focus on specific sections that address your current challenges. At the end of each chapter, you'll find an action plan to help you apply what you've learned. These plans offer step-by-step instructions so you can immediately put the book's concepts into practice.

By following the guidance in this book and engaging with the action plans, you'll create meaningful changes in your time management and productivity, leading to greater success in both your professional and personal life.

This book includes exclusive downloadable resources, detailed in the Appendices. To access them, visit www.impisimedia.com/resources. You'll need to register for a free account and enter the access code found in **Appendix B** to unlock the materials.

Chapter 1
Time Tracking and Analysis

"Time is what we want most, but what we use worst."
Michael Altshuler

Overview

Tracking time and analyzing how it is spent is fundamental to increasing personal productivity. By recording daily activities, individuals can identify patterns that reveal inefficiencies. This process allows for reducing time-wasting habits and enhancing focus on tasks that support personal and professional goals. The benefits of this practice are not just about productivity, but also about personal growth and fulfillment.

Understanding where time is lost or underutilized is essential for making informed decisions about time management. By analyzing tracked time, individuals can adjust their schedules to prioritize activities that align with their goals. This shift in focus can significantly affect both productivity and overall success.

In this section, we will delve into why time tracking and analysis are critical for personal growth. We will discuss practical strategies for accurately tracking time and analyzing the data gathered effectively. These strategies will help you manage your time more efficiently, enabling you to achieve your goals more effectively.

Through consistent tracking and thoughtful analysis, you can take control of your time, turning it into a valuable resource that drives success in both personal and professional endeavors.

Importance of Time Tracking and Analysis

Time is a precious resource, and how we manage it significantly influences our productivity and well-being. When we don't understand how our time is spent, prioritizing tasks effectively becomes difficult. Tracking time offers essential insights, showing us where our time goes. With this data, we can set better goals and make decisions that improve productivity.

Analyzing tracked time helps us spot areas needing adjustment. This process allows us to make strategic choices that enhance how we use our time. Effective time management, driven by accurate analysis, ensures we focus on activities that yield the best results.

Strategies for Time Tracking

Time tracking is the process of recording and analyzing how time is spent on various activities. It's essential for improving productivity, managing tasks, and achieving goals. By understanding where time goes, individuals can make informed decisions about how to use it more effectively. In this section, we'll explore different time-tracking tools and methods, along with their advantages and disadvantages.

Digital Time Tracking Tools

Toggl: Toggl is a popular time-tracking tool known for its simplicity and ease of use. It allows users to track time across multiple projects with a single click. Toggl provides detailed reports, making it easy to see where time is spent. However, its free version has limited features, and it may not integrate with all other software tools.

Pros:

- User-friendly interface.
- Provides detailed reports.
- Available across multiple platforms.

Cons:

- Limited features in the free version.
- It may not integrate with all software.

RescueTime: RescueTime automatically tracks how time is spent on digital activities, categorizing websites and applications. It helps users understand their productivity patterns by showing how much time is spent on work-related versus distracting activities. However, RescueTime might not be as effective for tracking non-digital tasks.

Pros:

- Automated time tracking.
- Provides insights into digital habits.
- It helps find distractions.

Cons:

- Limited to digital activities.
- The free version has fewer features.

Harvest: Harvest is a robust tool for time tracking, invoicing, and expense management. It's ideal for freelancers and small businesses that need to track billable hours. Harvest integrates with many project management tools, making it versatile. However, it may be too complex for individuals, only needing basic time tracking.

Pros:

- Integrates with project management tools.
- Supports invoicing and expense tracking.
- Suitable for teams and businesses.

Cons:

- May be too complex for individual use.
- Higher cost compared to simpler tools.

Clockify: Clockify is a free time-tracking tool that offers unlimited tracking for teams. It provides detailed reporting and integrates with various apps. However, its user interface can be overwhelming for beginners.

Pros:

- Free with unlimited tracking.
- Integrates with various apps.
- Provides detailed reports.

Cons:

- Complex user interface.
- Can be overwhelming for beginners.

Using a Journal or Spreadsheet

Time tracking doesn't always require digital tools. Many prefer using a journal or spreadsheet to manually log their activities. This method offers flexibility and can be customized to fit individual needs. It also allows for tracking non-digital tasks that digital tools might miss. However, it requires more effort to keep and analyze.

Pros:

- Flexible and customizable.
- Allows for non-digital task tracking.
- No need for an internet connection.

Cons:

- Time-consuming to keep.
- Requires manual analysis.

Automated Tracking of Digital Activities

Automated tracking involves using software that runs in the background, recording how time is spent on digital devices. These tools can track website visits, app usage, and even idle time.

Chrome's Clockify Time Tracker

Clockify's Chrome extension tracks time spent on websites and apps directly from the browser. It's ideal for those who spend a lot of time online. However, it doesn't track activities outside the browser.

Pros:

- Easy to use within Chrome.
- Tracks web-based activities.

Cons:

- Limited to browser activities.
- Doesn't track non-digital tasks.

RescueTime: As discussed earlier, RescueTime is another

effective tool for automated tracking, especially for identifying time-wasting activities online. It provides weekly reports that summarize productivity.

Pros:

- Automated tracking with detailed reports.
- Helps identify and reduce distractions.

Cons:

- Limited to digital activities.
- May not capture all productivity.

Toggl Track

Toggl Track offers a feature that automatically tracks time spent on specific apps and websites. It's useful for professionals who need to account for every minute spent online. However, like other tools, it doesn't track offline activities.

Pros:

- Tracks time automatically.
- Integrates with other productivity tools.

Cons:

- Limited to digital tasks.
- Doesn't track non-digital activities.

Setting Reminders or Alerts

Setting reminders or alerts can help ensure time tracking stays consistent. For example, you might set a timer to remind you to log your time every hour. This method works well for those who forget to track time or need a nudge to stay on task.

Examples:

- Use phone alarms to prompt hourly time logs.
- Set up calendar alerts to review and log daily activities.

Pros:

- Keeps you on track with time logging.
- Reduces the chance of missing logs.

Cons:

- Can be disruptive if overused.
- May become less effective over time.

Strategies for Time Analysis

Time analysis involves examining the data collected through time tracking to uncover insights that can improve productivity and effectiveness. It's a critical step in ensuring that time is spent wisely, supporting both personal and professional goals. In this section, we'll explore how to analyze time-tracking data, identify patterns, and make strategic adjustments to enhance productivity.

Understanding Time Analysis

Time analysis is the process of reviewing tracked time to find patterns, trends, and areas for improvement. By examining daily and weekly reports, you can gain insights into how your time is distributed across different tasks and activities. This information is invaluable for making informed decisions about how to better allocate your time, end inefficiencies, and focus on what matters most.

Reviewing Daily and Weekly Reports

Daily and weekly time reports provide a snapshot of how time is spent over specific periods. By reviewing these reports, you can identify patterns and trends in your work habits. For example, you might notice that certain tasks consistently take longer than expected, or that your productivity peaks at specific times of the day.

Look for recurring patterns in your time usage. Are there specific times when you're most productive? Are there activities that regularly consume more time than expected? Finding these patterns allows you to adjust your schedule to maximize productivity during peak periods and minimize time wasted on less productive tasks.

Categorize your tasks to understand where your time is going. Are you spending too much time on administrative work and not enough on high-impact tasks? Breaking down your activities into categories helps you see how much time is dedicated to each type of task, making it easier to prioritize and reallocate time where it's most needed.

Identify periods of high and low productivity. Productivity peaks often occur during times when energy levels are high, while valleys may coincide with fatigue or distractions. Understanding when these peaks and valleys occur can help you plan your day more effectively, scheduling important tasks during peak times and less critical activities during valleys.

Review your reports to spot recurring distractions or interruptions. These could be anything from frequent phone calls to unscheduled meetings. Recognizing these patterns allows you to address the root causes, such as setting boundaries or improving time management strategies to minimize disruptions.

Identifying Time Wasters

Time wasters are activities that consume time without contributing significant value. Common time wasters include excessive meetings, social media, and unnecessary multitasking.

While multitasking might seem efficient, it often leads to reduced productivity and lower-quality work. When you multitask, your attention is divided, making it harder to focus fully on any one task. Analyzing your time-tracking data can help you identify if multitasking is affecting your productivity. Look for patterns where multiple tasks are tried simultaneously and assess the impact on the quality and completion time of those tasks.

Consider the time spent checking emails. While necessary, frequent email checks can interrupt your workflow and reduce productivity. Analyzing your reports might reveal that limiting email checks to specific times of the day could free up valuable time for more important tasks.

Understanding Productivity Peaks and Valleys

Productivity peaks are periods when you are most focused and energetic, while valleys are times of low energy and motivation. These fluctuations are natural and can be influenced by several factors, including sleep, nutrition, and work environment.

Peaks typically occur when you are well-rested and mentally sharp, often in the morning or after a break. Valleys, on the other hand, may occur during post-lunch hours or when you've been working for an extended period without rest.

Use the insights from your time analysis to schedule important tasks during productivity peaks. During valleys, focus on less demanding tasks or take breaks to recharge. This approach ensures that you're using your most productive times for tasks that require the most focus and energy.

Evaluating Task Effectiveness

Analyzing the effectiveness of your tasks is crucial for aligning your time with your goals. Not all tasks contribute equally to your success, so it's important to identify those that have the most significant impact.

Review your tasks to decide which ones directly contribute to your overall goals. Tasks that generate the most value should be prioritized, while less impactful tasks may need to be delegated or minimized.

Based on your analysis, consider reallocating time from less valuable tasks to those that drive results. This might involve shifting your focus from routine administrative work to strategic planning or creative projects that align more closely with your goals.

Experimenting with Time Management Strategies

Time analysis is not just about looking back; it's also about planning ahead. Experimenting with different time management strategies can help you find the most effective approach for your needs.

Delegating tasks is one way to free up time for more important activities. Analyze which tasks can be delegated to others, allowing you to focus on high-impact work.

Establishing boundaries is essential for protecting your time. Whether it's setting specific times for meetings or limiting access to your workspace, clear boundaries help minimize interruptions and keep you on track.

Consider experimenting with time-blocking, where you dedicate specific blocks of time to certain tasks, or the Pomodoro technique, which involves working in focused bursts with short breaks. Analyzing the effectiveness of these strategies will help you refine your time management approach.

Section recap

In this section, we explored the importance of time tracking and analysis in improving productivity and achieving goals. We discussed various tools and methods for tracking time, from digital apps like Toggl and RescueTime to traditional journals and spreadsheets. Analysis of time-tracking data helps find patterns, uncover time wasters, and improve your daily schedule. Understanding productivity peaks and valleys, and evaluating the effectiveness of your tasks, allows you to align your time management with your goals. By experimenting with different strategies, such as delegation and setting boundaries, you can refine your approach to time management.

The building blocks of time management for improved productivity

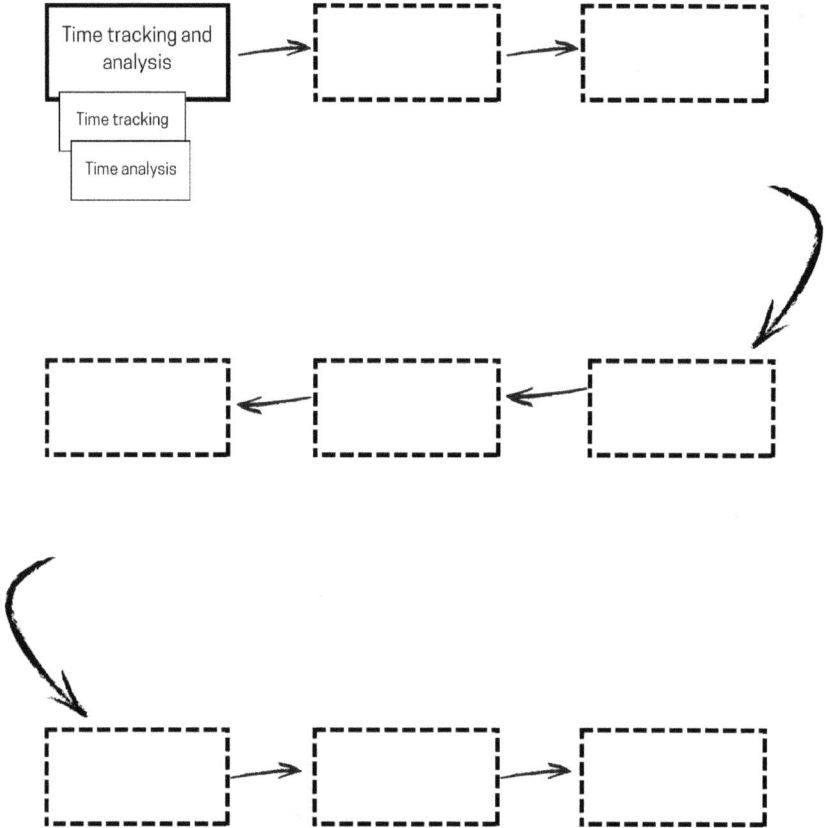

Action plan

- **Track Time:** Choose a tool or method that fits your needs (e.g., Toggl, journal).

- **Analyze Data:** Review daily and weekly reports to identify patterns and trends.

- **Identify Time Wasters:** Spot inefficiencies and avoid unnecessary tasks.

- **Improve Schedule:** Align high-impact tasks with your productivity peaks.

- **Experiment and Adjust:** Try different strategies like time-blocking and delegation.

Chapter 2
Effective Goal Setting and Prioritization

"The key is not to prioritize what's on your schedule, but to schedule your priorities."

Stephen Covey

Overview

In the business world, success often hinges on the ability to set clear goals and prioritize tasks effectively. Goal setting is the process of identifying what you want to achieve and establishing a plan to get there. It's about turning your vision into actionable steps that lead to tangible results. On the other hand, prioritization involves deciding which tasks are most important and allocating your resources accordingly.

This section will cover the essential principles of both goal setting and prioritization. You will learn how to define your objectives clearly and how to decide what needs to be done first to maximize your efforts. Moreover, we will delve into practical strategies to put these concepts into practice. By mastering goal setting and prioritization, you will be better equipped to navigate the complexities of business and achieve sustainable success.

Understanding Goal Setting

Goal setting is a fundamental process that lays the foundation for success in any endeavor. It involves defining specific, measurable goals you aim to achieve within a set time limit.

This process provides direction, motivation, and clarity, guiding your actions toward desired outcomes. Effective goal setting is not just about deciding what you want to achieve; it's about creating a roadmap to get there, ensuring that each step you take is purposeful and aligned with your broader vision.

SMART framework

One of the most widely recognized frameworks for setting effective goals is the SMART method. SMART stands for Specific, Measurable, Achievable, Relevant, and Time-bound. Each element plays a crucial role in transforming vague ambitions into actionable plans.

- **Specific**: Clearly defining your goals is the first step in the SMART process. Instead of setting broad or ambiguous goals, aim to be as detailed as possible. Specify what you want to achieve, why it's important, and how it will impact your overall mission. For example, rather than saying, "I want to increase sales," a specific goal would be, "I want to increase sales by 15% in the next quarter by expanding our online marketing efforts."

- **Measurable**: Once your goal is specific, it's essential to establish concrete criteria for measuring progress and success. This ensures that you can track your achievements and adjust as needed. Measurable goals offer a straightforward way to gauge whether you're on track or need to pivot. For example, if your goal is to improve customer satisfaction, you might measure success by aiming for a 10% increase in positive feedback on customer surveys.

- **Achievable**: While it's important to set ambitious goals, they must also be realistic. Consider your resources, capabilities, and constraints when defining your goals. An achievable goal stretches you but is still within the realm of possibility.

   Setting unattainable goals can lead to frustration and burnout, while realistic goals keep you motivated and focused. For instance, setting a goal to double your business revenue in a month may not be workable, but aiming for a 20% increase over six months could be more realistic.

- **Relevant**: Your goals should align with your values, priorities, and long-term aspirations. Relevance ensures that the goals you set matter to you and contribute to your overall vision. Ask yourself whether the goal is worth pursuing and how it fits into your broader objectives. For example, if your long-term goal is to become a leader in sustainable products, setting a short-term goal to reduce your company's carbon footprint would be relevant and aligned with that vision.

- **Time-bound**: Finally, setting a deadline or target date for achieving your goals is crucial. A time-bound goal creates a sense of urgency and accountability, encouraging you to take consistent action. Without a timeline, goals can become perpetually delayed. For example, committing to launch a new product by the end of the year gives you a clear time limit to work within and helps prioritize tasks.

Breaking down goals into milestones

In addition to using the SMART framework, breaking down larger goals into smaller, manageable milestones can significantly enhance your ability to achieve them. Large goals can feel overwhelming, but when you divide them into bite-sized tasks, they become more manageable and less daunting. This approach not only keeps your motivation high but also keeps momentum as you achieve each milestone.

Commit goals to paper

Writing down your goals is another powerful technique. Committing your goals to paper—or a digital document— reinforces your commitment and serves as a tangible reminder of what you're working toward. Whether you choose to document your goals in a journal, planner, or project management tool, having them in writing increases accountability and clarity.

Visualize success

Visualization is a technique often used by high achievers to mentally rehearse success. By picturing yourself achieving your goals, you can increase motivation and confidence. Visualization helps you focus on the positive emotions associated with achievement, making the process feel more real and attainable.

Review and adjust

Finally, regular review and adjustment of your goals are essential.

Life and circumstances change, and your goals should be flexible enough to adapt. Regularly assess your progress, decide if your goals are still relevant, and make any necessary adjustments. This adaptability ensures that your goals continue to align with your evolving priorities and remain within reach.

By understanding and applying these goal-setting techniques, you can lay a solid foundation for success. Whether you're aiming to grow your business, improve personal skills, or achieve any other objective, effective goal setting is the key to turning your ambitions into reality.

Effective Prioritization Strategies

Once you've clearly defined your goals, the next critical step is to prioritize tasks and activities. Prioritization is the art of identifying the most important and urgent tasks and giving your time and resources accordingly.

Effective prioritization ensures that you focus on what matters most, making progress toward your goals without getting sidetracked by less important activities. Below are some strategies for prioritization that can help you manage your tasks effectively.

ABCDE Method

The ABCDE method is a simple yet powerful way to prioritize tasks based on their importance and urgency. In this method, each task is assigned a letter (A, B, C, D, or E), reflecting its priority level.

- **A-tasks**: These are top priorities—tasks that must be completed because they have significant consequences if left undone. These tasks are often urgent and directly affect your most critical goals.

- **B-tasks**: While still important, B-tasks are less urgent than A-tasks. Completing them is necessary, but the consequences of delay are not as severe.

- **C-tasks**: These tasks are nice to do but not essential. They have little to no consequences if left incomplete, making them lower priorities.

- **D-tasks**: Tasks that can be delegated to others fall into this category. Delegation allows you to focus on higher-priority tasks while ensuring that necessary but less critical work gets done.

- **E-tasks**: These are tasks that can be eliminated or postponed without any negative impact. Finding and removing E-tasks from your to-do list frees up time for more important activities.

By categorizing tasks using the ABCDE method, you can ensure that your time and energy are focused on what truly matters, leading to greater efficiency and productivity.

Eisenhower Matrix

The Eisenhower Matrix, also known as the Urgent-Important Matrix, is a prioritization tool that helps you categorize tasks into four distinct quadrants based on their urgency and importance. This method allows you to decide where to focus your efforts most effectively.

High   Low

Urgency

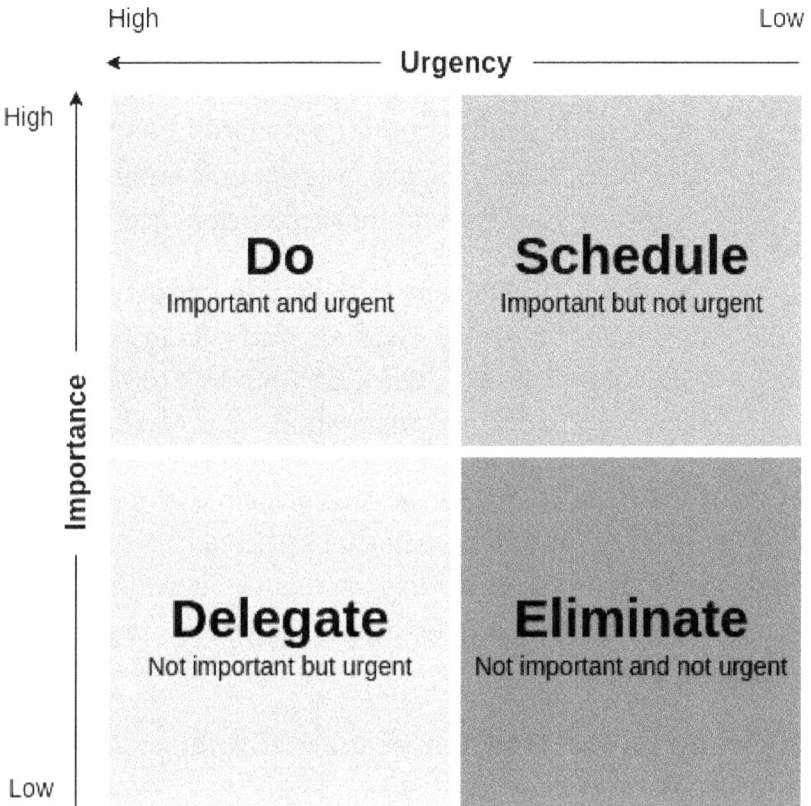

	Do Important and urgent	**Schedule** Important but not urgent
	Delegate Not important but urgent	**Eliminate** Not important and not urgent

- **Quadrant I: Urgent and Important**: Tasks in this quadrant require immediate attention and are crucial to achieving your goals. These tasks often involve deadlines or crises and should be addressed as soon as possible.

- **Quadrant II: Important but Not Urgent**: Tasks in this quadrant are key to long-term success but do not require immediate action. These include strategic planning, personal development, and relationship-building activities. Prioritizing these tasks helps prevent future crises and promotes steady progress toward your goals.

- **Quadrant III: Urgent but Not Important**: Tasks in this quadrant demand immediate attention but do not contribute significantly to your goals. These are often distractions or interruptions that can be minimized or delegated. Managing these tasks efficiently is crucial to protecting your time for more important activities.

- **Quadrant IV: Neither Urgent nor Important**: Tasks in this quadrant are timewasters and should be avoided or eliminated. These tasks do not contribute to your goals and can easily lead to procrastination.

By using the Eisenhower Matrix, you can gain clarity on what tasks need immediate attention, what tasks should be scheduled for later, and what tasks can be delegated or removed. This helps you focus on high-impact activities and avoid getting caught up in less important work.

For more on the Eisenhower matrix, refer to Appendix B: Resources.

Time Blocking

Time blocking is a productivity technique that involves giving specific blocks of time in your schedule for tasks or activities. This method helps ensure that important tasks receive the attention they deserve without being overshadowed by less critical activities.

To practice time blocking, start by identifying your most important tasks. Then, assign dedicated time slots in your daily or weekly schedule to work on these tasks. During these blocks, cut distractions and focus solely on the task at hand. For example, you might block out two hours every morning to work on a high-priority project, ensuring that this time is reserved exclusively for that work.

Time blocking not only helps you stay organized but also encourages deep focus and prevents multitasking, which can reduce efficiency. By setting aside uninterrupted time for your most important tasks, you increase the likelihood of completing them effectively and on time.

Eat That Frog

The concept of "eating the frog" comes from a famous quote by Mark Twain: "If it's your job to eat a frog, it's best to do it first thing in the morning." In this context, the "frog" stands for your most challenging or unpleasant task. Tackling this task first thing in the day can build momentum, boost confidence, and free up mental energy for the rest of your work.

When you "eat that frog," you address the hardest, most dreaded task before anything else. This approach prevents procrastination and ensures that your day starts with a sense of accomplishment. Once the biggest challenge is out of the way, the rest of your tasks will feel easier to manage.

Use Prioritization Tools

In today's digital age, many tools and techniques are available to help you prioritize tasks effectively. To-do lists, task management apps, and Kanban boards are just a few examples.

- **To-do lists**: These are simple but effective tools for organizing and ranking tasks according to their importance and urgency. A well-organized to-do list helps you stay on top of your responsibilities and ensures that nothing falls through the cracks.

- **Task management apps**: Digital tools like Trello, Asana, or Todoist offer advanced features for task prioritization. These apps allow you to set deadlines, track progress, and collaborate with others, making them particularly useful for managing complex projects.

- **Kanban boards**: Originally developed for manufacturing, Kanban boards are now widely used in various industries for task management. A Kanban board visually represents your tasks and helps you visualize your workflow and prioritize tasks based on their status.

Using these tools can enhance your ability to prioritize effectively, keeping you organized and focused on high-priority activities. Thet are discussed in more detail in the next section.

Section recap

Goal setting and prioritization are essential tools for anyone looking to achieve meaningful results. By establishing clear, realistic goals and prioritizing tasks based on their importance and urgency, you can ensure that your efforts align with your desired outcomes. This approach maximizes efficiency and helps you stay focused on what truly matters.

Whether you're aiming to grow a business, improve personal skills, or enhance your life, mastering these techniques will empower you to take control and reach your full potential. Start applying these strategies today to unlock greater productivity and success.

The building blocks of time management for improved productivity

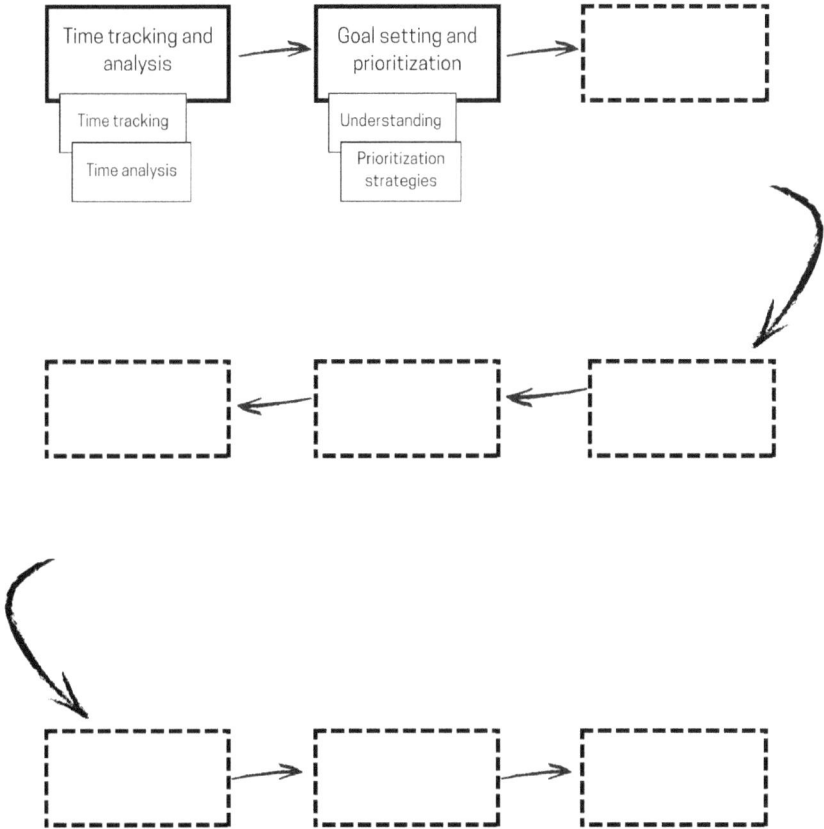

Time tracking and analysis	Goal setting and prioritization	
Time tracking	Understanding	
Time analysis	Prioritization strategies	

Action plan

To put your goal setting and prioritization strategies into practice, follow this step-by-step action plan. This will help you stay focused and make consistent progress toward your goals.

- Commit to Writing:

- Document your goals, tasks, and priorities in a journal, planner, or digital tool.

- Identify Big-Picture Goals:

- Clearly define your overarching goals (career, personal development, health, or business).

- Ensure each goal is Specific, Measurable, Achievable, Relevant, and Time-bound (SMART).

- Break Down Goals into Actionable Tasks:

- Divide each big-picture goal into smaller, manageable tasks.

- Assign target dates for completing each task.

- Prioritize Daily:

- Begin each day or week by reviewing your goals and identifying top-priority tasks.

- Use the ABCDE method or Eisenhower Matrix to rank tasks based on importance and urgency.

- Focus on completing A-tasks (most important) first.

- Time Block High-Value Activities:

- Allocate specific blocks of time in your schedule for high-priority tasks.

- Ensure these blocks are free from distractions.

- Review and Adjust:

- Regularly assess your progress toward your goals.

- Adjust your tasks, priorities, and timelines as needed.

- Stay flexible and adapt to changes in circumstances.

- Visualize Success:

- Spend a few minutes each day visualizing the completion of your top-priority tasks.

- Imagine the positive outcomes and feelings associated with achieving your goals.

- Track Progress and Celebrate Milestones:

- Monitor your progress toward each goal.

- Celebrate when you reach key milestones to keep motivation!

Chapter 3
Task management systems

"Your mind is for having ideas, not holding them."
David Allen

Overview

Effective task management is the backbone of productivity, particularly in a world filled with distractions and competing priorities. Building on the earlier discussion of prioritization, understanding task management systems is crucial. These systems are designed to help you stay organized, reduce stress, and focus on what truly matters.

Whether you're running a business or managing personal projects, the right task management system can make all the difference. From simple to-do lists to sophisticated task management apps and Kanban boards, each tool offers unique benefits. This section will provide an overview of various task management systems, helping you choose the one that aligns best with your needs. By implementing an effective system, you can enhance your productivity, stay on top of your tasks, and achieve your goals with greater efficiency.

To-do lists

To-do lists are a fundamental tool in task management. They provide a clear and straightforward way to organize and track tasks.

A to-do list is essentially a checklist of tasks that you need to accomplish. These lists can take many forms, from simple handwritten notes to digital lists on task management apps. The format may vary depending on personal preferences and the complexity of the tasks at hand. Some people prefer a traditional pen-and-paper approach, while others use apps that offer advanced features like reminders, due dates, and task sharing.

Let's discuss how to make the most of a to-do list.

Create a Master List

- The first step in making the most of a to-do list is to create a master list. This list should include all tasks that need to be completed, regardless of their size or importance. The purpose of a master list is to ensure that nothing is overlooked.

- By compiling everything into a single list, you gain a comprehensive view of your responsibilities. This approach not only helps in organizing tasks but also reduces the mental burden of remembering everything.

Prioritize Tasks

- Once you have your master list, the next step is to prioritize the tasks. Not all tasks are equally important or urgent. Prioritizing allows you to focus on the most critical tasks first. Techniques like the ABCDE method, where tasks are categorized from A (most important) to E (least important), or the Eisenhower Matrix, which categorizes tasks based on urgency and importance, can be particularly useful. By prioritizing, you ensure that your time and energy are directed towards tasks that have the greatest impact.

Break Down Tasks

- Large tasks can be overwhelming, which often leads to procrastination. To combat this, break down larger tasks into smaller, more manageable sub-tasks. This makes it easier to start and complete the task.

- For example, instead of listing "Write a report," you could break it down into "Research topics," "Create an outline," and "Draft sections." This approach not only makes the task seem less daunting but also allows you to track progress incrementally, giving you a sense of accomplishment as you complete each sub-task.

Use Categories or Labels

- Organizing tasks by categories or labels can further enhance the effectiveness of your to-do list. By grouping similar tasks together, you can streamline your workflow. For instance, you might label tasks as "Work," "Personal," or "Errands."

This method allows you to focus on specific types of tasks at different times, increasing your efficiency. It also helps in quickly finding related tasks, which can be combined, saving time and reducing context switching.

Review and Update Regularly

- A to-do list is only effective if it is kept up to date. Regularly reviewing and updating your list is crucial. This includes adding new tasks, marking off completed ones, and re-prioritizing tasks as needed.

- Regular reviews help you stay on track and ensure that your list reflects your current goals and responsibilities. It also offers an opportunity to reassess priorities, allowing you to adjust your focus as circumstances change.

  By keeping your to-do list current, you ensure that it stays a reliable tool for managing your tasks and achieving your goals.

Kanban boards

Kanban boards are powerful tools for visualizing and managing tasks. Originating from the manufacturing industry, particularly from Toyota's production system in the 1940s, Kanban is a Japanese term meaning "signboard" or "visual signal."

The system was developed to improve efficiency and control the flow of work on the assembly line. Today, Kanban boards are widely used across various industries, from software development to personal productivity, because of their simplicity and effectiveness in managing workflows.

Who Benefits Most from Kanban Boards?

Kanban boards are highly beneficial for teams and individuals who need to manage tasks and projects efficiently. Teams working in agile environments, such as software development, often find Kanban boards invaluable. These boards help in visualizing work, limiting work in progress (WIP), and showing bottlenecks in the process.

However, Kanban boards are not limited to teams; individuals can also use them for personal task management. Freelancers, students, and even busy parents can use Kanban boards to keep track of their responsibilities and ensure that nothing falls through the cracks.

Forms of Kanban Boards

Kanban boards can take various forms, ranging from simple physical boards to elaborate electronic versions. The most basic form of a Kanban board is a physical pin board or whiteboard, where tasks are represented as sticky notes or index cards. This method is tactile and offers a tangible way to interact with tasks.

Kanban Board

An uncomplicated form of a digital board can be created in Excel and spreadsheets can be customized to suit diverse needs.

On the other hand, digital Kanban boards, like Trello or Jira, offer more advanced features, such as task assignment, deadlines, and collaboration tools. These electronic versions are especially useful for remote teams, as they allow real-time updates and easy access from anywhere.

Whether physical or digital, the core principle of visualizing work stays the same.

Using Kanban Boards Effectively

To use Kanban boards effectively, start by **creating columns**. These columns typically represent various stages of the workflow, such as "To Do," "In Progress," and "Done." You can customize the columns based on your specific needs, adding stages like "Waiting for Approval" or "Testing" if necessary.

Next, **add tasks as cards**. Each task or project should be represented as a card that is placed in the appropriate column.

The card should include all relevant information, such as task details, deadlines, and any attached files or links.

As work progresses, **move cards between columns** to reflect the status of each task. This movement provides a clear visual sign of progress and helps you quickly see what is being worked on and what is completed.

One key aspect of Kanban is to **limit work-in-progress (WIP)**. By setting a limit on the number of tasks that can be in the "In Progress" column at any one time, you can ensure that work is completed before new tasks are started. This helps prevent bottlenecks and keeps the workflow smooth.

Additionally, **use labels** to categorize tasks. Labels can show priority, type of work, or any other relevant categorization. This feature is particularly useful in digital Kanban boards, where color-coded labels can quickly convey essential information at a glance.

Keep It Simple

One of the strengths of Kanban boards is their simplicity. Avoid overcomplicating your board with too many columns, tasks, or labels. The goal is to keep a clear and straightforward visualization of your workflow. Regularly review your board to ensure it is still a useful tool, not a burden.

For more on Kanban boards, including a free Excel template, refer to Appendix B: Resources.

Task management apps

Task management apps have become indispensable tools in

our digital age, offering a range of features designed to help individuals and teams organize, prioritize, and complete tasks efficiently. These apps go beyond the basic to-do list by incorporating various functionalities like reminders, collaboration tools, progress tracking, and more.

They provide a centralized platform where tasks can be managed from start to finish, making them ideal for both personal productivity and team coordination. With the vast array of task management apps available today, finding the right one can significantly improve your workflow and help you stay on top of your responsibilities.

Todoist

Todoist is one of the most popular task management apps available. It offers a clean, intuitive interface that allows users to easily create and organize tasks. Todoist supports task prioritization, enabling users to assign various levels of urgency to tasks.

Additionally, it offers project templates, recurring tasks, and integrations with other apps like Google Calendar and Slack. One of its standout features is the ability to set up nested tasks and subtasks, which helps in breaking down larger projects into more manageable pieces. Todoist also includes productivity tracking, allowing users to see their progress over time through visual graphs and charts.

Trello

Trello is a highly visual task management app that uses the Kanban board system. It allows users to create boards for different projects, with each board having lists and cards that represent tasks and stages of work. Trello's drag-and-drop interface makes it easy to move tasks between various stages, such as "To Do," "In Progress," and "Done." Users can attach files, set due dates, and collaborate with team members on tasks.

Trello's power-ups, which are integrations with other apps and services, enhance its functionality by adding features like calendar views, automation, and advanced reporting. This flexibility makes Trello a favorite for both individual users and teams.

Asana

Asana is a robust task management app designed for teams. It offers a wide range of features that facilitate project management, task assignment, and team collaboration. Users can create tasks, assign them to team members, set deadlines, and track progress all within the app.

Asana's timeline feature is particularly useful for managing complex projects, as it provides a visual overview of how tasks and deadlines intersect. Additionally, Asana supports task dependencies, allowing users to specify which tasks need to be completed before others can begin. The app also integrates with many other tools, such as Slack, Dropbox, and Google Drive, making it a comprehensive solution for team productivity.

Microsoft To Do

Microsoft To Do is a simple yet powerful task management app that is ideal for both personal and professional use. It integrates seamlessly with other Microsoft products, such as Outlook and OneNote, allowing users to manage their tasks across multiple platforms. Microsoft To Do offers features like task prioritization, reminders, and the ability to create recurring tasks.

One of its unique features is the My Day function, which allows users to focus on tasks they want to complete each day, helping to manage daily priorities effectively. The app's clean and minimalist design makes it easy to use, while its integration with the Microsoft ecosystem enhances its functionality for those already using other Microsoft tools.

Notion

Notion is more than just a task management app; it's an all-in-one workspace that combines notes, databases, task management, and collaboration tools. Users can create customizable workspaces that include tasks, notes, and project management tools all in one place. Notion's flexibility allows users to design their workflow according to their needs, whether that's a simple to-do list or a complex project management system.

It supports rich media, allowing users to embed images, videos, and files within their tasks and notes. Notion also enables collaboration, making it a great tool for teams that need to manage tasks and share information in a centralized platform.

Conclusion

Task management apps offer a wide range of features to help users stay organized and productive. Whether you prefer the simplicity of Microsoft To Do, the visual approach of Trello, or the all-in-one functionality of Notion, there is an app suited to your needs. By exploring these options and understanding their unique features, you can find the right tool to enhance your workflow and achieve your goals.

Section recap

This section provided an in-depth look at different task management tools that can help you stay organized and productive.

We started with to-do lists, which offer a simple and effective way to capture and prioritize tasks. Next, we explored Kanban boards, a visual tool that helps manage workflows by moving tasks through various stages of completion. Finally, we examined task management apps like Todoist, Trello, Asana, Microsoft To Do, and Notion. These apps offer advanced features for managing tasks, from setting priorities and deadlines to facilitating team collaboration.

Each tool has unique strengths, making it crucial to choose the one that best suits your needs. By understanding and applying these tools, you can significantly enhance your ability to manage tasks efficiently, whether for personal projects or team-based work.

So, choose your preferred task management system, get organized, and start making progress towards your goals today!

The building blocks of time management for improved productivity

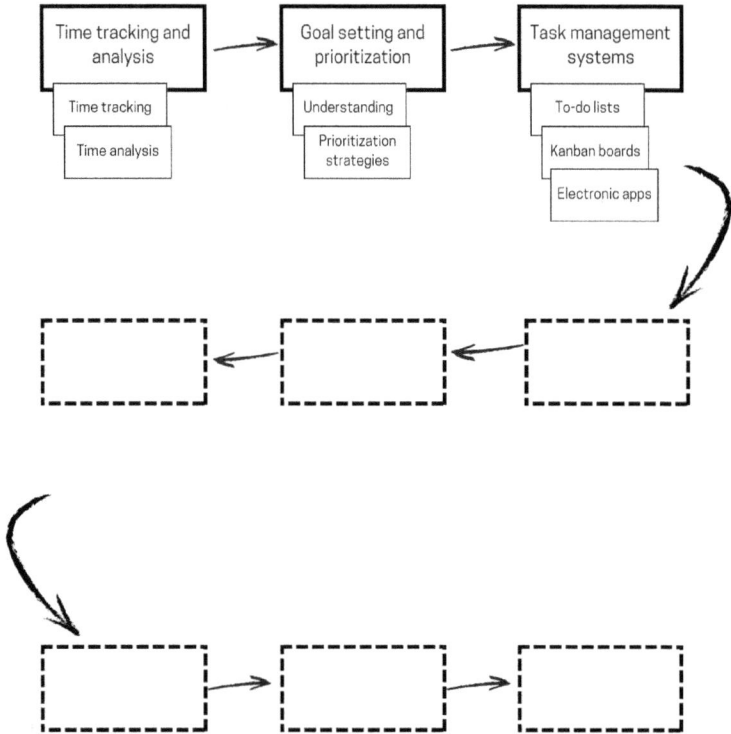

```
┌─────────────────┐      ┌─────────────────┐      ┌─────────────────┐
│ Time tracking and│ ──▶  │ Goal setting and │ ──▶  │ Task management │
│    analysis      │      │  prioritization  │      │    systems      │
└─────────────────┘      └─────────────────┘      └─────────────────┘
  ┌─────────────┐          ┌─────────────┐          ┌─────────────┐
  │Time tracking│          │Understanding│          │ To-do lists │
  └─────────────┘          └─────────────┘          └─────────────┘
    ┌─────────────┐          ┌─────────────┐          ┌─────────────┐
    │Time analysis│          │Prioritization│         │Kanban boards│
    └─────────────┘          │  strategies  │         └─────────────┘
                             └─────────────┘            ┌─────────────┐
                                                        │Electronic apps│
                                                        └─────────────┘
```

```
┌- - - - - -┐      ┌- - - - - -┐      ┌- - - - - -┐
│           │ ◀──  │           │ ◀──  │           │
└- - - - - -┘      └- - - - - -┘      └- - - - - -┘

┌- - - - - -┐      ┌- - - - - -┐      ┌- - - - - -┐
│           │ ──▶  │           │ ──▶  │           │
└- - - - - -┘      └- - - - - -┘      └- - - - - -┘
```

Action plan

To put this section into action, start by thinking about your requirements, then choosing a task management tool that aligns with that.

Chapter 4
Mastering productivity with time blocking

"The secret of your future is hidden in your daily routine."
Mike Murdock

Overview

In today's fast-paced world, time management is crucial. Time blocking, a powerful productivity tool, helps you take control of your schedule. It involves dividing your day into blocks of time, each dedicated to specific tasks. By doing so, you focus on one task at a time, reducing distractions and increasing efficiency.

This section will explore the concept of time blocking. We will examine its benefits, such as enhanced focus, better task prioritization, and reduced stress. Additionally, we will delve into techniques for implementing effective time blocks, ensuring you make the most of your day. Finally, we'll discuss real-life applications, showing how successful people use time blocking to achieve their goals.

By mastering this technique, you can transform how you manage your time, leading to greater productivity and a more balanced life.

Understanding time blocking

Time blocking is a productivity method where you allocate specific blocks of time to different tasks or activities throughout your day. This technique helps you structure your day in a way that allows you to focus entirely on one task at a time, thereby improving efficiency and reducing stress.

The concept of time blocking is not new; it has its roots in ancient practices, such as the way monks organized their days. However, it gained popularity in the modern world through the work of productivity experts like Cal Newport and Elon Musk, who have successfully used this method to manage their time effectively.

Set clear objectives

To begin with time blocking, the first step is to set clear objectives. You need to know exactly what you want to achieve during your day. This requires identifying your most important tasks and understanding your overall goals.

When you have a clear sense of what needs to be done, you can begin to allocate time in a way that maximizes productivity. Setting clear objectives ensures that your time is spent on activities that align with your goals, rather than getting involved in less important tasks.

Find time blocks

Once your objectives are set, the next step is to find time blocks within your schedule. This involves reviewing your daily routine and finding periods that can be dedicated to focused work. It's important to consider when you are most productive. Some people are more alert in the morning, while others do their best work in the afternoon or evening.

By aligning your most important tasks with your peak productivity periods, you can make the most of your time. Finding the right time blocks is crucial for ensuring that your day is structured efficiently.

Allocate time for specific tasks

After finding time blocks, the next step is to allocate time for specific tasks. This is where the true power of time blocking comes into play. Each block of time is assigned a particular task or activity. This could range from work-related tasks, like drafting a report, to personal activities, such as exercising or reading.

By assigning specific tasks to each time block, you end the need to multitask, allowing you to focus fully on the task at hand. This level of focus helps increase the quality of your work and reduces the time needed to complete tasks.

Minimizing interruptions and distractions

Minimizing interruptions and distractions is another critical aspect of time blocking. In today's world, it's easy to get sidetracked by notifications, emails, and other distractions. During your designated time blocks, it's essential to create an environment that allows for uninterrupted work.

This might involve turning off notifications, closing unnecessary tabs on your computer, or even informing colleagues or family members that you are not to be disturbed during certain periods. By minimizing interruptions, you ensure that each time block is used as efficiently as possible.

Review and adjust

Finally, it's important to review and adjust your time blocks as needed. Life is unpredictable, and your schedule may need to change from day to day. Regularly reviewing your time blocks allows you to adjust based on what is working and what isn't.

If you find that certain tasks are taking longer than expected, or that you are consistently interrupted during specific time blocks, it might be necessary to tweak your schedule. The key is to remain flexible while keeping a structured approach to your day.

In conclusion, time blocking is a powerful tool for managing your time more effectively. By setting clear objectives, finding and allocating time blocks, minimizing distractions, and regularly reviewing your schedule, you can take control of your day.

This method not only helps you do more but also reduces stress by providing a clear structure for your day. Whether you are managing a business, working on personal projects, or simply trying to make the most of your time, time blocking can be an invaluable strategy for achieving your goals.

Benefits of time-blocking

Time blocking offers many benefits that can significantly enhance your productivity and efficiency. By structuring your day into focused segments, you gain control over your time, leading to a more organized and effective approach to tasks.

Below, we discuss six key benefits of time blocking that can transform how you manage your day.

Improved focus

One of the primary benefits of time blocking is improved focus. When you dedicate a specific block of time to a single task, your mind can fully engage with that activity. This deep level of focus is difficult to achieve when multitasking or when distractions are constantly interrupting your flow.

Time blocking allows you to enter a state of "deep work," where you can concentrate on complex tasks without interruption. This focused approach not only increases the quality of your work but also reduces the time needed to complete it.

Better time management

Another significant benefit is better time management. Time blocking forces you to think critically about how you allocate your hours. By planning your day in advance, you become more aware of how much time you spend on each activity. This awareness helps you avoid overcommitting or underestimating the time required for certain tasks.

With time blocking, you can create a realistic schedule that ensures all important tasks are completed without unnecessary stress. This method also helps you identify time-wasting activities, allowing you to eliminate them and make better use of your time.

Increased productivity

Increased productivity is a direct result of better focus and time management. When you dedicate uninterrupted time to specific tasks, you can do more in less time. The act of blocking time itself serves as a commitment to completing a task, which can motivate you to work more efficiently.

Additionally, knowing that you have set time aside for each task reduces the temptation to procrastinate. As a result, your overall productivity increases, allowing you to achieve your goals faster and more effectively.

Reduced stress

Time blocking also plays a crucial role in reducing stress. A well-structured day can alleviate the overwhelming feeling that comes with a long to-do list. When you see your tasks laid out in manageable time blocks, the day feels less chaotic. You know exactly when and how each task will be tackled, which reduces anxiety.

Furthermore, time blocking can help you build in breaks and downtime, ensuring that you don't burn out. This structured approach provides a sense of control and order, which can significantly lower stress levels.

Enhanced work-life balance

Another benefit of time blocking is enhanced work-life balance. By allocating specific blocks of time for work-related tasks and personal activities, you create boundaries between different areas of your life. This separation ensures that work doesn't spill over into your personal time, allowing you to fully disconnect and recharge.

Additionally, time blocking can help you prioritize personal activities, such as exercise, hobbies, or spending time with family. This intentional scheduling ensures that you keep a healthy balance between work and personal life, leading to greater overall well-being.

Better decision-making

Finally, time blocking encourages better decision-making. When your day is planned out in advance, you reduce the need to make constant decisions about what to do next. This reduction in decision fatigue allows you to focus your mental energy on more important tasks.

By allocating specific times for decision-making tasks, such as planning or strategizing, you can approach these activities with a fresh mind. Time blocking thus helps you make more thoughtful and effective decisions, further enhancing your productivity.

In summary, time blocking is a powerful tool for improving focus, managing time more effectively, increasing productivity, reducing stress, enhancing work-life balance, and making better decisions. By adopting this method, you can take control of your day and achieve your goals with greater ease and efficiency.

Techniques for effective time-blocking

Mastering time blocking requires understanding and implementing a few key techniques. By using these methods, you can tailor time blocking to fit your personal and professional needs.

Below, we discuss several techniques that can help you effectively block your time and maximize your productivity.

Use themes

One effective technique is to theme your days. This involves assigning a specific theme or focus to each day of the week. For example, Monday could be dedicated to meetings and planning, while Tuesday might focus on creative work. By theming your days, you group similar tasks together, which helps streamline your workflow.

Themed days reduce the mental strain of switching between unrelated tasks and allow you to immerse yourself fully in one type of work. For instance, if you're a writer, you might dedicate an entire day to research and another to writing. This approach helps you stay focused and makes it easier to manage your time.

Use tools or apps

Using time blocking tools or apps is another technique that can enhance your time management. Tools like Google Calendar, Microsoft Outlook, and Todoist are popular options that offer customizable time blocking features. These apps allow you to visually map out your day, set reminders, and adjust your schedule as needed.

For example, Google Calendar allows you to create color-coded blocks for different tasks, making it easy to see your schedule at once. Microsoft Outlook's calendar feature also lets you set time blocks directly from your emails, helping you stay organized.

Todoist, on the other hand, combines task management with time blocking, allowing you to set deadlines and prioritize tasks within specific time slots. By using these tools, you can efficiently manage your time and stay on track with your goals.

Start small

If you're new to time blocking, it's important to start small. Begin by blocking out just one or two key tasks each day. For instance, you might start by blocking 30 minutes for email management in the morning and another 30 minutes for planning your day. As you become more comfortable with the process, you can gradually increase the number of time blocks you use.

Starting small prevents you from feeling overwhelmed and allows you to ease into the habit of time blocking. Over time, you'll find it easier to structure your entire day using this method.

Be realistic

Being realistic about your time blocks is crucial to ensuring success. It's tempting to try and fit as many tasks as possible into your day, but overloading your schedule can lead to burnout and frustration. For example, if you know that a particular task usually takes an hour, don't try to squeeze it into a 30-minute time block. Instead, allocate enough time for each task, leaving room for unexpected delays. By being realistic, you create a schedule that is achievable and sustainable, leading to better long-term productivity.

Include buffer time

Including buffer time between your time blocks is another essential technique. Buffer time allows for flexibility in your schedule, giving you space to manage unexpected interruptions or to transition between tasks.

For instance, if you've blocked out time for back-to-back meetings, include a 10–15-minute buffer between each meeting. This buffer time can be used to process what was discussed, take notes, or simply relax for a moment before moving on to the next task. Including buffer time reduces the stress of feeling rushed and ensures that your schedule stays manageable.

In summary, effective time blocking requires a combination of strategic techniques. Theming your days, using time blocking tools, starting small, being realistic, and including buffer time are all methods that can help you master this productivity tool. By implementing these techniques, you can create a time-blocking system that works for you, leading to increased efficiency and a more organized approach to your daily tasks.

Real life applications

Time blocking is a versatile technique that can be applied to various aspects of daily life, from managing work projects to ensuring quality family time. Below, we explore how time blocking can be effectively used in different real-life scenarios.

Work projects

One of the most common applications of time blocking is for work projects. Whether you're managing a large project or handling day-to-day tasks, time blocking can help you stay on track. For example, if you're working on a project with multiple stages, you can block out time each day for specific tasks like research, writing, and editing.

This approach ensures that each aspect of the project receives the attention it needs, reducing the likelihood of rushing through tasks at the last minute. Time blocking allows you to break down complex projects into manageable chunks, making it easier to meet deadlines and maintain high-quality work.

Daily routine

Another practical use of time blocking is in organizing your daily routine. By scheduling time blocks for activities like exercise, meal preparation, and household chores, you can ensure that these essential tasks don't get overlooked.

For instance, you might block out 30 minutes in the morning for a workout, followed by 15 minutes for a healthy breakfast. In the evening, you can set aside time for cleaning or other household responsibilities. Time blocking helps create a balanced routine that supports both your personal and professional life, making it easier to manage your time and reduce stress.

Meetings and appointments

Time blocking is also highly effective for managing meetings and appointments. Instead of allowing meetings to disrupt your entire day, you can choose specific time blocks for them. For example, you might reserve the first two hours of your morning for focused work and block off the late morning or early afternoon for meetings.

This approach helps prevent meetings from taking over your day and ensures that you have uninterrupted time to complete your most important tasks. Additionally, by setting aside specific times for appointments, you can avoid the last-minute scramble to fit everything in, leading to a more organized and less stressful schedule.

Personal time

Personal development is another area where time blocking can make a significant impact. Whether you're learning a new skill, reading, or engaging in a hobby, blocking out time for personal growth ensures that these activities remain a priority. For instance, you might dedicate an hour each evening to learning a new language or improving a professional skill. By consistently allocating time to personal development, you can make steady progress toward your goals, even with a busy schedule.

Family time

Finally, time blocking can be a powerful tool for ensuring quality family time. In today's busy world, it's easy for work and other obligations to encroach on family life. By blocking out specific times for family activities, such as dinners, game nights, or outings, you can ensure that you spend meaningful time with your loved ones. For example, you might reserve Sunday afternoons for family outings or set aside an hour each evening for family dinners. Time blocking helps create boundaries between work and family life, allowing you to be fully present during these important moments.

In conclusion, time blocking is a flexible and practical tool that can be applied to various aspects of life. Whether you're managing work projects, organizing your daily routine, handling meetings and appointments, focusing on personal development, or spending time with family, time blocking can help you make the most of your time. By using this technique, you can create a more balanced, productive, and fulfilling life.

Section recap

In this section, we explored the concept of time blocking and its powerful impact on productivity. We began by understanding what time blocking is, tracing its origins, and discussing how it structures your day for maximum efficiency. We then examined the many benefits, including improved focus, better time management, and reduced stress, all of which contribute to a more balanced and productive life.

We also delved into practical techniques for implementing time blocking, such as theming your days, using digital tools, and being realistic with your schedule. Finally, we looked at real-life applications of time blocking, from managing work projects to ensuring quality family time. By mastering these techniques, you can take control of your time and achieve your goals more effectively.

The building blocks of time management for improved productivity

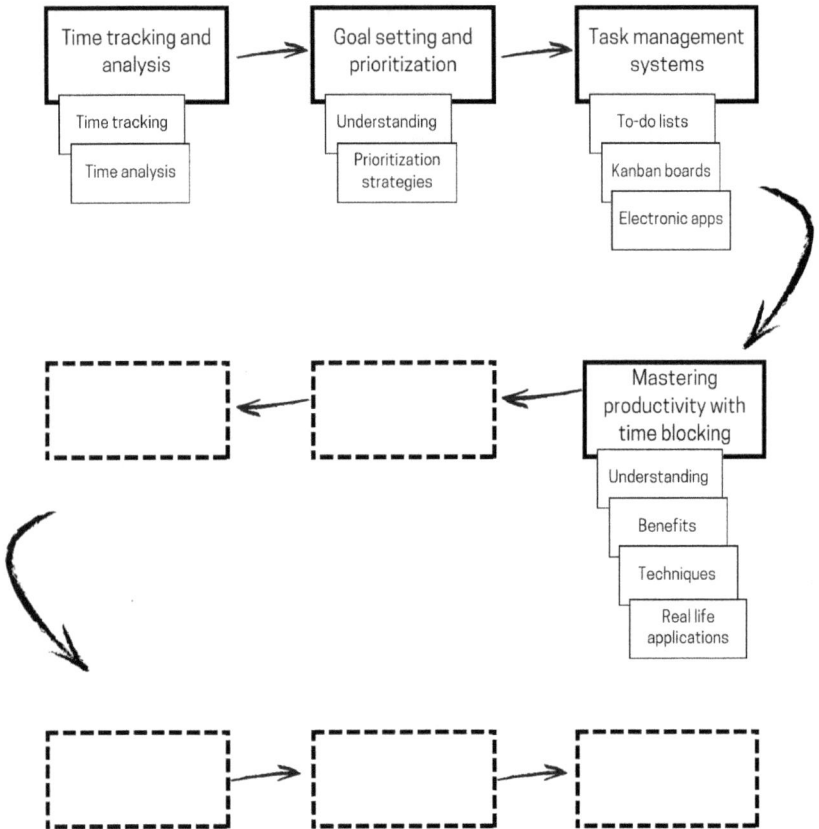

Action plan

To put this section into action, you can do the following:

- Follow the steps discussed in "Understanding time blocking".

- Study the suggested techniques and choose which ones to apply.

Chapter 5
Mastering focus and concentration

"The ability to concentrate and to use time well is everything. Success in any endeavor requires single-minded attention to detail and total concentration."

Willie Sutton

Overview

In this section, we delve into the critical elements of mastering focus and concentration. Understanding these concepts is essential for anyone aiming to excel in a business environment.

We will explore the nature of focus—what it is and why it matters. Additionally, we'll examine practical strategies that can help you improve your focus. These include methods for minimizing distractions, both in your environment and within your own mind.

We will also cover techniques to enhance your concentration, enabling you to sustain your attention on tasks that require deep, sustained effort.

Mastering these skills will empower you to work more effectively, make better decisions, and ultimately achieve your business goals. This section serves as a guide to harnessing your mental faculties, ensuring that you stay sharp, focused, and on course in your entrepreneurial journey.

Understanding focus and concentration

Focus and concentration are fundamental skills for anyone looking to succeed in business. Though often used interchangeably, they serve distinct functions.

Focus is the ability to direct your attention towards a specific task or goal. It involves filtering out distractions and keeping a sharp vision of what you need to achieve. Concentration, on the other hand, is the sustained effort needed to maintain that focus over time. It is the mental endurance that allows you to stay engaged with a task until it is completed.

Mastering these skills leads to improved performance in almost every aspect of your work. When you can focus, your productivity increases because you spend less time switching between tasks. Concentration allows you to dive deeper into tasks, leading to more thorough and thoughtful outcomes. Together, these skills help you complete work more efficiently, saving both time and energy.

Additionally, focus and concentration are crucial for enhanced learning and memory. When you concentrate fully on a subject, you absorb information more effectively. This deep level of engagement strengthens your memory, making it easier to recall vital details later.

Whether you're learning a new skill or developing a business strategy, these skills ensure that the knowledge you gain is retained and easily accessible when needed.

Moreover, mastering focus and concentration can significantly reduce stress and anxiety. Distractions and multitasking often lead to feelings of overwhelm, as unfinished tasks pile up. By focusing on one task at a time and seeing it through to completion, you can manage your workload more effectively. This approach reduces the mental clutter that contributes to stress, allowing you to keep a calmer, more controlled mindset.

Strategies for improving focus

Improving focus requires practice and discipline. It's not something that happens overnight, but with consistent effort, you can significantly enhance your ability to concentrate on tasks that matter. Below are key strategies to help you strengthen your focus.

Set Clear Goals

The first step in improving focus is setting clear, specific goals. When you know exactly what you need to achieve, it's easier to direct your attention toward it. Vague or broad goals can lead to confusion and a lack of direction, making it difficult to stay focused. Instead, break down your goals into specific, actionable steps. This clarity will serve as a guide, helping you stay on track and avoid distractions.

Break Tasks into Manageable Chunks

Large tasks can be overwhelming and lead to procrastination. To counter this, break tasks into smaller, more manageable chunks. By dividing work into bite-sized pieces, you reduce the mental burden and make it easier to keep focus.

Each completed chunk gives you a sense of accomplishment, which can boost motivation and help you stay engaged. This method also allows you to tackle complex projects step by step, ensuring steady progress without feeling overwhelmed.

Use Time Blocking

Time blocking is a powerful technique for improving focus - we discussed it in depth in Section 5. During these blocks, you commit to working on one task without interruptions. By allocating dedicated time slots, you create a structured environment that minimizes distractions.

This approach helps you manage your time more effectively, ensuring that you give each task the attention it deserves. Additionally, time blocking can help prevent burnout by balancing work periods with breaks, allowing you to recharge.

Practice Mindfulness

Mindfulness is another effective strategy for enhancing focus. It involves being fully present in the moment, paying attention to your thoughts and surroundings without judgment.

By practicing mindfulness, you can train your mind to stay focused on the task at hand, rather than getting lost in distractions.

Techniques such as deep breathing, meditation, or simply taking a few moments to center yourself can improve your ability to concentrate. Over time, mindfulness can increase your mental resilience, making it easier to maintain focus even in challenging situations.

Limit Multitasking

Multitasking is often seen as a way to get more done, but it can hinder focus and productivity. When you try to juggle multiple tasks at once, your attention is divided, leading to mistakes and slower progress. Instead, focus on one task at a time.

By giving your full attention to a single task, you can complete it more efficiently and with higher quality. Limiting multitasking reduces mental fatigue and helps you stay sharp throughout your workday.

In conclusion, improving focus is a skill that requires intentional effort. By setting clear goals, breaking tasks into manageable chunks, using time blocking, practicing mindfulness, and limiting multitasking, you can cultivate a sharper, more focused mind. These strategies will not only enhance your productivity but also improve the quality of your work, setting you on a path toward greater success.

Techniques for minimizing distractions

Distractions can significantly hinder your productivity and prevent you from reaching your full potential. They fragment your attention, slow down progress, and increase the likelihood of errors. Minimizing distractions is crucial for maintaining focus and achieving your goals. Here are effective techniques to help you stay on track.

Create a Distraction-Free Environment

The first step in minimizing distractions is to create a workspace that supports focus. This means eliminating unnecessary clutter and organizing your surroundings in a way that reduces visual and auditory interruptions.

Consider arranging your desk so that everything you need is within reach and remove items that are not essential to the task at hand. Noise-canceling headphones can help block out background noise, while a clean, organized space can create a sense of calm, making it easier to concentrate. The environment you work in plays a critical role in your ability to focus, so take the time to set it up thoughtfully.

Set Boundaries with Technology

Technology is one of the most common sources of distraction in the modern workplace. The constant ping of notifications and the lure of social media can easily pull you away from your work. To combat this, set strict boundaries with technology.

Turn off non-essential notifications on your phone and computer during work hours. You can also use apps that limit your access to distracting websites or that block notifications altogether. Choosing specific times to check emails and messages can also help you stay focused on your tasks without the constant interruption of incoming communication.

Set Boundaries with Others

It's important to set clear boundaries with those around you, especially if you work in a shared space or from home. Let others know when you need uninterrupted time to focus. This might involve communicating your work schedule to family members or coworkers and asking them to avoid disturbing you during those periods.

You can also use visual cues, such as closing your door or wearing headphones, to signal that you're in a focused work mode. Setting these boundaries helps create a respectful environment where your need for concentration is understood and honored.

Use Productivity Tools

There are many productivity tools available that can help you minimize distractions and stay on task. Tools like time-tracking apps can help you monitor how you spend your time and identify areas where distractions might be creeping in. Task management apps allow you to organize your to-do list and set priorities, ensuring that you stay focused on the most important tasks.

Some tools even use techniques like the Pomodoro method, which breaks work into focused intervals with short breaks in between. These tools provide structure to your workday, making it easier to keep focus and reduce the impact of distractions.

Regular Breaks

Taking regular breaks is essential for keeping focus over extended periods. When you work without breaks, your concentration wanes, making you more susceptible to distractions. Schedule short breaks throughout your day to recharge and refocus. During these breaks, step away from your work environment and engage in activities that relax your mind.

Whether it's a quick walk, stretching, or deep breathing exercises, these breaks help clear your mind and prepare you for the next period of focused work. Regular breaks prevent burnout and keep your mind sharp, allowing you to keep an elevated level of productivity.

In conclusion, minimizing distractions is key to improving focus and productivity. By creating a distraction-free environment, setting boundaries with technology and others, using productivity tools, and taking regular breaks, you can significantly reduce the impact of distractions on your work. Implementing these techniques will help you stay focused, complete tasks more efficiently, and achieve your goals with greater ease.

Strategies for maintaining concentration

Maintaining concentration over extended periods can be challenging, especially in a world filled with distractions and competing demands. However, with the right strategies, you can improve your ability to stay focused and engaged with your tasks. Here are effective techniques to help you maintain concentration.

Practice Attention Control

Attention control is the ability to direct your focus to where it is needed most and to resist distractions that may arise. This skill is crucial for maintaining concentration. Start by consciously deciding where you want your attention to go and then practice keeping it there. When you notice your mind wandering, gently bring it back to the task at hand.

Over time, this practice will strengthen your ability to concentrate. You can also use techniques like mental labeling, where you identify and name distractions as they arise, which can help you dismiss them more easily. Building attention control is like exercising a muscle—the more you practice, the stronger it becomes.

Stay Physically Active

Physical activity is not only good for your body but also for your mind. Regular exercise has been shown to improve concentration by increasing blood flow to the brain, which enhances cognitive function. Incorporate physical activity into your daily routine, whether it's a brisk walk, yoga, or a workout at the gym. Even short bursts of activity can help refresh your mind and improve your ability to concentrate.

Staying active also reduces stress and anxiety, which are common barriers to maintaining concentration. By keeping your body fit, you support your brain's ability to stay focused and alert.

Proper Diet and Hydration

What you eat and drink plays a significant role in your ability to concentrate. A balanced diet rich in nutrients fuels your brain, helping you keep concentration throughout the day. Foods high in omega-3 fatty acids, antioxidants, and complex carbohydrates can boost brain function.

Additionally, staying hydrated is essential for cognitive performance. Dehydration can lead to fatigue and difficulty concentrating. Make sure to drink plenty of water to keep your energy levels stable. By taking care of your body's nutritional needs, you create a solid foundation for sustained concentration.

Practice Active Listening

Active listening is a powerful strategy for improving concentration, especially in situations that require interaction with others. When you practice active listening, you fully engage with the speaker, focusing on their words, tone, and body language. This level of engagement helps you stay present in the conversation and improves your ability to retain information.

To practice active listening, avoid interrupting the speaker, ask clarifying questions, and paraphrase what you've heard to ensure understanding. This technique not only enhances concentration but also strengthens your communication skills, making it a valuable tool in both personal and professional settings.

In conclusion, maintaining concentration is a skill that can be developed with intentional practice and healthy habits. By practicing attention control, staying physically active, maintaining a proper diet and hydration, and practicing active listening, you can significantly improve your ability to concentrate.

———◆○◆———

Section recap

In this section, we explored the critical skills of focus and concentration, essential for achieving success in any business environment.

We began by understanding the distinction between focus and concentration, emphasizing their role in improving performance, increasing efficiency, enhancing learning and memory, and reducing stress. We then delved into practical strategies for improving focus, such as setting clear goals, breaking tasks into manageable chunks, using time blocking, practicing mindfulness, and limiting multitasking.

Furthermore, we discussed techniques for minimizing distractions, including creating a distraction-free environment, setting boundaries with technology and others, using productivity tools, and taking regular breaks. Finally, we examined strategies for maintaining concentration, such as practicing attention control, staying physically active, maintaining a proper diet and hydration, and practicing active listening.

By applying these strategies, you can cultivate a sharper, more focused mind, leading to greater productivity and success.

The building blocks of time management for improved productivity

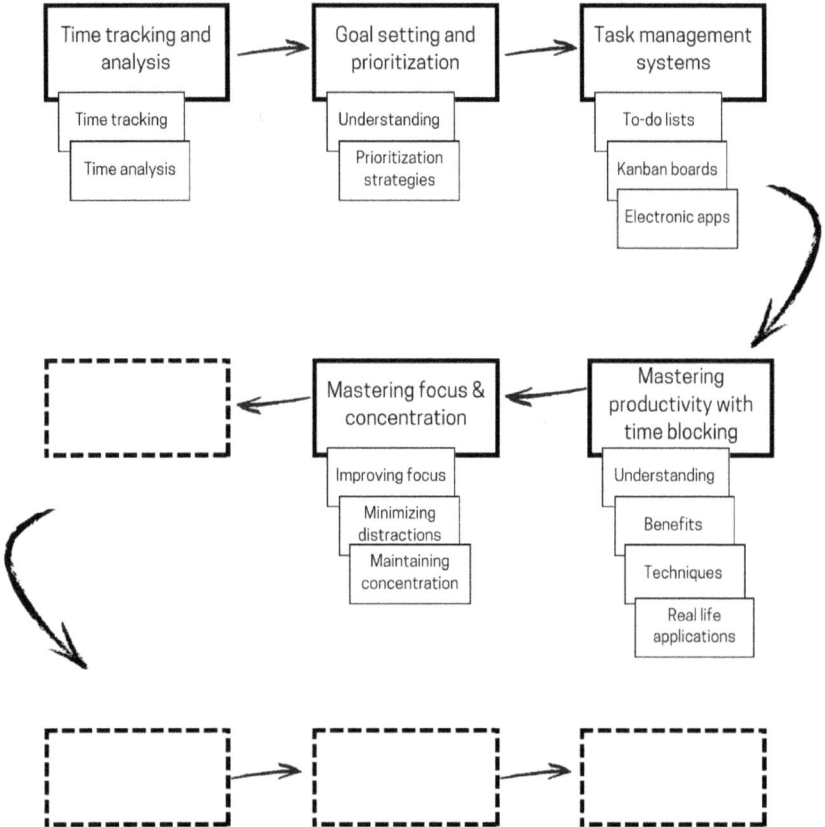

Time tracking and analysis	Goal setting and prioritization	Task management systems
Time tracking	Understanding	To-do lists
Time analysis	Prioritization strategies	Kanban boards
		Electronic apps

	Mastering focus & concentration	Mastering productivity with time blocking
	Improving focus	Understanding
	Minimizing distractions	Benefits
	Maintaining concentration	Techniques
		Real life applications

Action plan

To put this section into action, decide which strategies or techniques to use for each of the following:

1. To improve focus

2. To minimize distractions

3. To improve concentration

Chapter 6

Energy management in productivity

"Your energy is unique. Embrace it. Use it wisely. Make it count."

Robin Sharma

Overview

Energy management is a critical yet often overlooked aspect of personal productivity. While time management involves allocating specific hours to tasks, energy management focuses on the quality and intensity of those hours.

The key to unlocking optimal performance lies in understanding your natural energy levels and how they fluctuate throughout the day. Unlike time, which is constant and finite, energy is a dynamic resource that varies in intensity and availability.

Recognizing and aligning tasks with your natural energy rhythms can significantly enhance your productivity and well-being.

Understanding energy management

Your energy levels are influenced by many factors, including sleep patterns, diet, exercise, and even genetics. Everyone has a unique energy rhythm, meaning that the best time for high-effort tasks will differ from person to person. Some people are morning-oriented, finding that their energy peaks shortly after they wake up. This period is ideal for tackling complex or high-priority tasks that require deep focus and mental clarity. For others, the morning may be a time to ease into the day, with energy levels peaking later in the afternoon or evening.

A common pattern for many individuals includes a morning peak in energy, followed by an early afternoon slump. This midday drop in energy often coincides with the body's natural circadian rhythm and can be worsened by factors such as a heavy lunch or dehydration. During this slump, it's more challenging to maintain concentration, and productivity may decrease. However, recognizing this pattern allows you to plan accordingly, scheduling less demanding tasks during this time to avoid frustration and inefficiency.

Fortunately, after this early afternoon dip, many people experience a recovery in their energy levels. This late afternoon resurgence is an excellent time to complete ongoing projects or tackle tasks that require moderate focus. As the evening approaches, most people naturally begin to wind down. This phase is characterized by a gradual decline in energy as the body prepares for rest. It's a good time for less demanding tasks or relaxation, allowing you to recharge for the next day.

While these patterns are common, they are by no means universal. Some individuals, known as night owls, find that their peak energy levels occur in the evening or late at night. These people may perform their best work after most others have already begun to wind down for the day. Understanding and respecting your unique energy rhythm, whether it aligns with or deviates from the typical pattern, can help you structure your day more effectively.

Understanding your energy levels is not just about recognizing when you feel most awake or alert. It's about acknowledging the ebb and flow of your physical, mental, and emotional energy throughout the day and using that awareness to manage your tasks more efficiently. By aligning your most demanding tasks with your high-energy periods and reserving less intensive work for lower-energy times, you can maximize your productivity while minimizing stress and burnout.

In conclusion, energy management is about more than just getting through the day; it's about thriving by working in harmony with your natural rhythms. By understanding your energy levels, you can optimize your day, ensuring that you not only complete your tasks but also maintain a healthy balance between productivity and well-being.

Strategies for maximizing productivity with energy management

Now that we understand natural energy levels, we can use this knowledge to maximize productivity. Energy management is about more than just knowing when you have the most energy. It's about aligning your most critical tasks with your peak energy times. By doing this, you can work more efficiently and achieve better results.

The first strategy is to find your peak energy times. These are the moments in your day when you feel most alert, focused, and energized. To identify these times, pay attention to when you naturally feel the most productive. For many, this might be in the morning after a good night's sleep, while for others, it could be later in the day. Once you've pinpointed these peak periods, you can plan your high-energy tasks accordingly.

Matching these peak times with high-energy tasks is the next step. High-energy tasks are those that require concentration, creativity, or problem-solving. By tackling these tasks when your energy is at its highest, you can complete them more efficiently. For example, if your peak time is in the morning, you might choose to work on complex projects during this period, leaving simpler tasks for later.

Scheduling low-energy tasks strategically is essential. These tasks are less demanding and can be done when your energy is lower. For instance, answering emails or organizing files can be scheduled during your early afternoon slump. This approach ensures that every part of your day is productive, even when your energy levels dip.

Short breaks throughout the day can help you recharge and maintain consistent energy levels. These breaks can include a quick walk, deep breathing exercises, or simply stepping away from your work. Regular breaks prevent burnout and keep your energy levels stable, enabling you to maintain productivity throughout the day.

Practicing energy-boosting habits is crucial. These habits include maintaining a balanced diet, staying hydrated, exercising regularly, and getting enough sleep. Good habits support your energy levels, making it easier to manage them effectively. Simple changes like drinking more water or incorporating a short workout into your routine can significantly affect your daily energy levels.

Your workspace should be organized, comfortable, and free of distractions. Good lighting, a comfortable chair, and minimal clutter can help you keep focus and energy. Additionally, consider adding plants or personal touches to make your environment more inviting and energizing.

Finally, it's important to experiment and adjust. What works for someone else may not work for you. Be open to trying different strategies and adjusting them based on your experience. Track your energy levels, tasks, and productivity to see what combinations yield the best results. This process of experimentation and adjustment is key to mastering energy management.

By understanding your natural energy levels and applying these strategies, you can maximize your productivity. Energy management is an ongoing process, but with practice, you can learn to harness your energy effectively and achieve your goals more efficiently.

Section recap

In this section, we explored the concept of energy management and its crucial role in enhancing productivity.

Understanding your natural energy levels is the first step. By identifying peak energy times, you can align high-energy tasks with those moments, ensuring maximum efficiency. We also discussed the importance of scheduling low-energy tasks during periods of lower vitality, taking strategic breaks to recharge, and practicing energy-boosting habits.

Additionally, we highlighted the significance of improving your environment to support focus and energy. Finally, we emphasized the need for experimentation and adjustment to find the best strategies for your unique energy patterns. Mastering energy management allows you to work smarter, maintain consistent productivity, and improve overall well-being.

The building blocks of time management for improved productivity

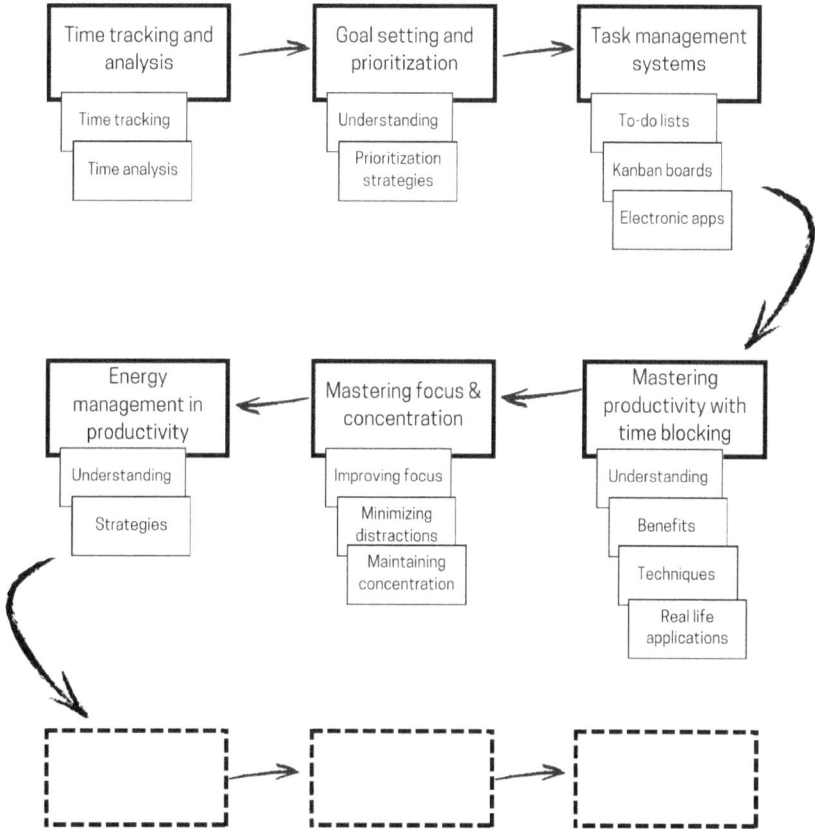

```
┌─────────────────┐      ┌─────────────────┐      ┌─────────────────┐
│ Time tracking and│ ──→  │ Goal setting and │ ──→  │ Task management │
│    analysis      │      │  prioritization  │      │     systems     │
└─────────────────┘      └─────────────────┘      └─────────────────┘
   Time tracking           Understanding             To-do lists
                           Prioritization
   Time analysis           strategies                Kanban boards

                                                     Electronic apps
```

```
┌─────────────────┐      ┌─────────────────┐      ┌─────────────────┐
│     Energy      │ ←──  │ Mastering focus &│ ←──  │    Mastering    │
│  management in  │      │  concentration   │      │ productivity with│
│  productivity   │      │                  │      │  time blocking  │
└─────────────────┘      └─────────────────┘      └─────────────────┘
   Understanding           Improving focus           Understanding
                           Minimizing
   Strategies              distractions              Benefits
                           Maintaining
                           concentration             Techniques

                                                     Real life
                                                     applications
```

```
┌ ─ ─ ─ ─ ─ ┐      ┌ ─ ─ ─ ─ ─ ┐      ┌ ─ ─ ─ ─ ─ ┐
│           │ ──→  │           │ ──→  │           │
└ ─ ─ ─ ─ ─ ┘      └ ─ ─ ─ ─ ─ ┘      └ ─ ─ ─ ─ ─ ┘
```

Action plan

To put this section into action, you can do the following:

- List the seven strategies for maximizing productivity with energy management.

- Apply these strategies in chronological order.

Chapter 7

Thriving under pressure: stress management

"There is no such thing as a stress-free life. No evidence has ever been presented which suggests that a stress-free life can ever be achieved. Stress can be managed, relieved and lessened, but never eliminated."

Gudjon Bergmann

Overview

Stress is a universal experience, affecting people in all occupations. Whether you're managing a business, balancing a demanding job, or handling personal responsibilities, stress is a constant companion.

Understanding the nature of stress is crucial for anyone looking to maintain mental and emotional well-being. In this section, we'll explore the common sources of stress and provide strategies to manage it effectively. These strategies include practical tools like time management and mindfulness practices. The goal is not just to cope with stress but to thrive, using it as a catalyst for personal growth and success.

Understanding the impact of stress on productivity

Stress is a psychological and physiological response to challenging or demanding situations. It triggers the body's "fight or flight" response, releasing hormones like cortisol and adrenaline. While this response can be beneficial in short bursts, prolonged stress can have detrimental effects on both mental and physical health.

In the workplace or personal life, the impact of stress on productivity is profound. Understanding these impacts can help you recognize when stress is becoming a barrier to success and take steps to mitigate its effects.

Cognitive function

One of the most immediate impacts of stress is impaired cognitive function. Under stress, your brain's ability to process information and make decisions diminishes. This occurs because stress hormones interfere with the brain's prefrontal cortex, which handles critical thinking, problem-solving, and decision-making.

As a result, tasks that would normally be simple become challenging, leading to frustration and further stress. Over time, chronic stress can even lead to more severe cognitive issues, such as memory loss and difficulty concentrating.

Motivation

Stress also significantly decreases motivation. When you're stressed, the brain's reward system becomes less responsive, making it harder to find the drive to complete tasks. This decrease in motivation can lead to procrastination, missed deadlines, and a general decline in productivity. It can create a vicious cycle, where the stress of falling behind leads to even greater stress, making it increasingly difficult to regain focus and motivation.

Errors and mistakes

Another critical impact of stress on productivity is the increase in errors and mistakes. When you're stressed, your attention to detail diminishes, and you become more prone to making careless errors. This is particularly concerning in high-stakes environments where accuracy is essential. The increased likelihood of mistakes not only slows down your progress but can also damage your reputation and lead to costly consequences. The stress of dealing with these mistakes can compound the problem, leading to even more errors in the future.

Resilience and health

Reduced resilience is another significant consequence of stress. Resilience refers to your ability to bounce back from setbacks and adapt to challenges. When stressed, your capacity for resilience diminishes, making it harder to recover from difficulties. This can lead to a sense of overwhelm and helplessness, further reducing productivity. In a workplace setting, reduced resilience can also affect teamwork, as stressed individuals may struggle to support their colleagues effectively.

Beyond these impacts, stress can also lead to physical health problems, which further affect productivity. Chronic stress is linked to conditions such as hypertension, heart disease, and weakened immune function. These health issues can lead to increased absenteeism and reduced ability to perform at your best, both of which negatively affect productivity. Additionally, the stress-health connection creates a feedback loop, where health problems worsen stress, leading to even greater productivity losses.

Creativity

In addition to the direct effects on cognitive function, motivation, errors, and resilience, stress can also harm your creativity. Creativity thrives in environments where the mind is free to explore innovative ideas without pressure. However, stress constrains thinking, making it harder to come up with innovative solutions or think outside the box. In professions that rely on creativity and innovation, this can be particularly damaging, leading to stagnation and a lack of progress.

Managing stress effectively is crucial for maintaining productivity in both personal and professional settings. By recognizing the signs of stress and understanding its impacts, you can take proactive steps to mitigate these effects. Remember, stress is not an inevitable part of life, but rather a challenge that can be managed with the right strategies.

Coping strategies for managing stress

Coping strategies are methods or techniques that individuals use to manage and reduce stress. These strategies help you deal with stressful situations and maintain your mental and emotional well-being.

Effective coping strategies can prevent stress from overwhelming you and ensure that it does not negatively affect your productivity or quality of life. Developing a personalized set of coping strategies is essential for navigating the inevitable challenges that life presents.

Meditation

One of the most effective coping strategies is mindfulness meditation. Mindfulness involves focusing on the present moment and accepting it without judgment. Regular mindfulness practice can help reduce stress by allowing you to detach from anxious thoughts and ground yourself in the here and now. This technique can improve your overall mental health and enhance your ability to manage stress.

Exercise

Regular physical activity helps release endorphins, which are natural mood boosters. Exercise also helps reduce levels of the body's stress hormones, such as adrenaline and cortisol. Whether it's a brisk walk, a yoga session, or a more intense workout, incorporating exercise into your routine can significantly reduce stress and improve your resilience.

Time management

Time management is another crucial coping strategy. Poor time management can lead to unnecessary stress, as tasks pile up and deadlines loom. By organizing your time effectively, you can reduce the pressure you feel and approach your tasks with a clear mind. Prioritizing tasks, breaking them into manageable chunks, and setting realistic deadlines are all ways to improve your time management skills and reduce stress.

Social support

Talking to friends, family, or colleagues about what you're going through can provide emotional relief and offer new perspectives on your situation. A strong support network can help you feel understood and less isolated, making it easier to cope with stressful situations. Whether it's a casual chat or a deeper conversation, connecting with others can be a powerful antidote to stress.

Relaxation

Relaxation techniques such as deep breathing, progressive muscle relaxation, or guided imagery can be highly effective. These techniques help calm the mind and body, reducing the physical symptoms of stress, such as a racing heart or tense muscles.

Practicing relaxation techniques regularly can help you stay calm and composed, even in high-pressure situations.

Healthy diet

A balanced diet provides your body with the nutrients it needs to function optimally, which can help you cope with stress more effectively. Foods rich in omega-3 fatty acids, antioxidants, and vitamins can boost your mood and energy levels, making it easier to manage stress.

Avoiding excessive caffeine, sugar, and processed foods can also help prevent stress from spiraling out of control.

Sleep

Sleep hygiene is more important than most people consider it to be. Lack of sleep can worsen stress, leading to a vicious cycle of sleepless nights and heightened anxiety. Establishing a regular sleep schedule, creating a relaxing bedtime routine, and ensuring your sleep environment is conducive to rest can help improve the quality of your sleep. Good sleep hygiene can make you more resilient to stress and improve your overall well-being.

Many of the strategies we've covered in previous sections, such as time management and mindfulness, can already contribute to reducing stress. By integrating these techniques into your daily life, you create a solid foundation for managing stress effectively. Remember, the key to coping with stress is not just to manage it but to thrive despite it. With the right strategies, you can turn stress into a powerful motivator rather than a debilitating force.

Case study: Rising above the challenge

At 46, Sarah found herself at a crossroads. Recently divorced, she was the sole provider for her two teenage children, both in high school. To make matters worse, she had just lost her job, a position she had held for over a decade. The thought of re-entering the job market filled her with dread. Instead, Sarah decided to use her skills as an experienced writer and editor and start a freelancing career from home. While the flexibility of freelancing seemed ideal, the uncertainty of this new venture quickly overwhelmed her.

Within weeks, Sarah secured a few clients. She was thrilled at first, but the demands of quick turnaround times, combined with her worries about the children and the need to build a solid reputation, pushed her stress levels to new heights. She found herself working late into the night, sacrificing sleep to meet deadlines and ensure her clients were satisfied. The constant pressure to deliver stellar work left her feeling drained and anxious, teetering on the brink of burnout.

Recognizing that she couldn't continue down this path, Sarah decided to take control of her situation. The first coping technique she introduced was **time management**. She began by setting clear boundaries between her work and personal life. She established a strict schedule, dedicating specific hours to work, family time, and self-care. By prioritizing tasks and breaking them into manageable chunks, Sarah found that she could meet deadlines without sacrificing her well-being.

Next, Sarah turned to **mindfulness meditation** to manage her anxiety. She started with just ten minutes a day, focusing on her breath and letting go of her racing thoughts. Over time, this practice helped her stay grounded, even when the demands of her work seemed overwhelming. Mindfulness allowed her to approach each task with a calm, focused mind, reducing the feelings of panic that had previously consumed her.

Physical exercise became another crucial part of Sarah's routine. Realizing that sitting at her desk for hours was worsening her stress, she committed to daily walks. These walks not only boosted her mood but also gave her a much-needed break from the screen, helping to clear her mind and improve her productivity when she returned to work.

Sarah also sought **social support** by reconnecting with friends and joining online communities of fellow freelancers. Sharing her experiences with others who understood her struggles provided her with emotional relief and practical advice. This support network became a source of encouragement, helping her feel less isolated on her journey.

Finally, Sarah embraced **relaxation techniques** such as deep breathing exercises and progressive muscle relaxation. These practices helped her release the physical tension that built up in her body throughout the day. By incorporating these techniques into her routine, she could unwind and recharge, preventing stress from taking a toll on her health.

Over time, these coping strategies transformed Sarah's approach to freelancing. What had once been a source of overwhelming stress became a fulfilling career. She found herself thriving, not just surviving. Her productivity improved, her clients were happy, and most importantly, she was able to provide for her children while maintaining her well-being. Sarah's story is a testament to the power of methodically applying coping strategies to not only manage stress but to flourish in the face of adversity.

Section recap

In this section, we explored the profound impact that stress can have on productivity. We discussed how stress impairs cognitive function, decreases motivation, and increases errors, all of which can hinder success. Additionally, we examined effective coping strategies, including mindfulness, exercise, and time management, which can help manage stress and enhance resilience.

The case study of Sarah illustrated how these techniques can be applied in real-life situations, showing the importance of a proactive approach to stress management. By understanding stress and implementing these strategies, you can not only cope with challenges but also thrive under pressure.

The building blocks of time management for improved productivity

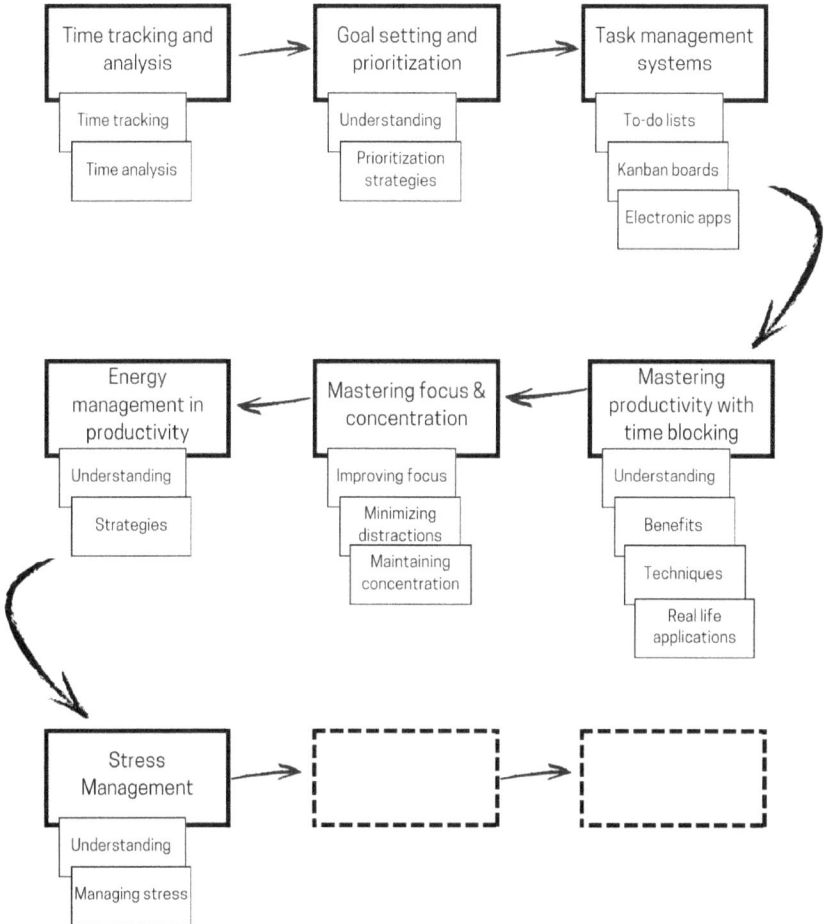

Time tracking and analysis	Goal setting and prioritization	Task management systems
Time tracking	Understanding	To-do lists
Time analysis	Prioritization strategies	Kanban boards
		Electronic apps

Energy management in productivity	Mastering focus & concentration	Mastering productivity with time blocking
Understanding	Improving focus	Understanding
Strategies	Minimizing distractions	Benefits
	Maintaining concentration	Techniques
		Real life applications

Stress Management		
Understanding		
Managing stress		

Action plan

To put this section into action, you can do the following:

- List the seven coping strategies for managing stress.

- Decide with which to start, and which ones to add later.

Chapter 8
Conquering procrastination

"It's the job that's never started and takes longest to finish."

JRR Tolkien

Overview

Procrastination is a common challenge for employees and entrepreneurs alike, especially when facing daunting tasks. It can hinder progress and, if not managed, lead to missed opportunities.

In this section, we will explore what procrastination is and why it happens. We will then discuss practical strategies to overcome it, helping you to stay on track and achieve your business goals. Additionally, we'll delve into methods for avoiding burnout, ensuring that your drive and passion remain strong.

Finally, we will examine a real-life case study that shows how conquering procrastination can lead to success. This overview sets the stage for a deeper understanding of the topic and equips you with actionable tools to manage your time effectively.

Understanding procrastination

Procrastination is the act of delaying or postponing tasks, often to the point where it becomes counterproductive. It's a common challenge that affects many people, regardless of their experience or discipline.

Understanding procrastination involves recognizing that it's not just about laziness or poor time management. It's often rooted in deeper psychological factors, such as fear of failure, perfectionism, or even anxiety. External factors like a lack of motivation or overwhelming workloads can also contribute to procrastination. These elements create a complex web that makes it difficult to start or complete tasks, even when the stakes are high.

It's essential to understand procrastination because of its significant impact on productivity. When you delay tasks, you not only lose valuable time but also reduce the quality of your work. The pressure to complete tasks last minute can lead to rushed decisions, errors, and subpar results. This reduction in productivity can be costly, especially in a business environment where efficiency and quality are crucial.

Additionally, procrastination can affect your well-being. The stress and anxiety that come with putting off tasks can lead to burnout, decreased satisfaction, and even mental health issues. Over time, the guilt and frustration from procrastination can erode your confidence and create a negative feedback loop, making it harder to break the habit.

One of the most challenging aspects of procrastination is how it can form a vicious cycle. When you procrastinate, you often feel guilty or stressed, which in turn makes it harder to start the next task. This cycle can become self-perpetuating, leading to chronic procrastination and a persistent sense of being overwhelmed.

By understanding the root causes of procrastination and its broader impacts, you can begin to develop strategies to overcome it. This awareness is the first step towards breaking the cycle and regaining control over your time and productivity.

Strategies for overcoming procrastination

Understanding procrastination is crucial for overcoming it effectively. Recognizing the underlying causes allows you to address the problem at its root, rather than merely treating the symptoms.

It's important to remember that while overcoming procrastination is challenging, it is by no means impossible. With the right strategies and techniques, you can break free from the habit and enhance both your productivity and well-being.

Some of the techniques or strategies to overcome procrastination were already discussed in earlier sections, but for the sake of completeness will be mentioned again. Let's discuss eight strategies that you can apply.

Pomodoro technique

One powerful technique is the Pomodoro Technique. This method involves breaking your work into 25-minute intervals, known as

"Pomodoros," followed by a short break. After completing four Pomodoros, take a longer break. This approach helps maintain focus while preventing burnout, making large tasks feel more manageable.

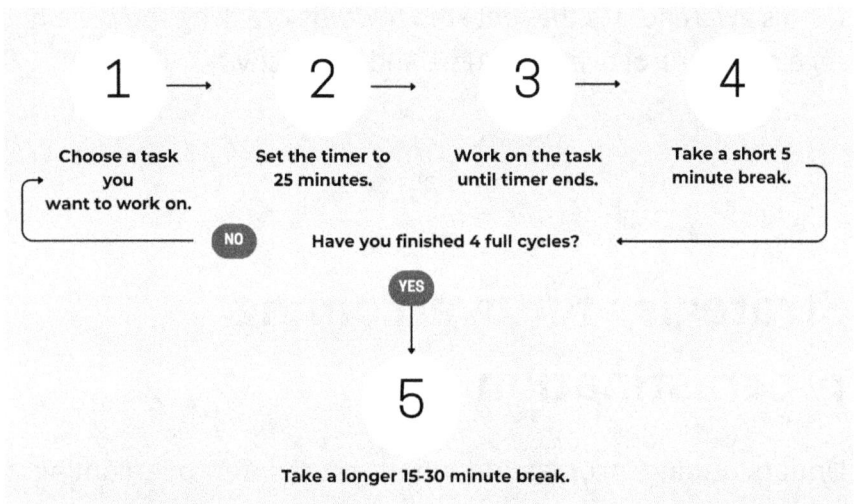

1 → **2** → **3** → **4**

Choose a task you want to work on.

Set the timer to 25 minutes.

Work on the task until timer ends.

Take a short 5 minute break.

NO   Have you finished 4 full cycles?

YES

5

Take a longer 15-30 minute break.

Goal setting

Set clear, achievable goals for each day, week, or project. Break down larger tasks into smaller, actionable steps. This not only makes the task less overwhelming but also provides a sense of accomplishment as you check off each item. Writing down your goals and revisiting them regularly can keep you motivated and on track.

Prioritization

Prioritization is key. Use techniques like the Eisenhower Matrix to categorize tasks by urgency and importance. Focus on high-priority tasks first, ensuring that you're working on what truly matters. By tackling these tasks early, you reduce the temptation to procrastinate on more critical work.

Eliminate distractions

Eliminating distractions is essential. Identify what typically distracts you—whether it is social media, emails, or noisy environments—and take steps to minimize these interruptions. For example, consider using website blockers during work hours or setting specific times to check your emails. Creating a dedicated workspace can also help in keeping focus.

Time management

Time management plays a significant role in overcoming procrastination. Implementing a schedule or routine helps in creating a structure that makes it easier to start and complete tasks. Use tools like planners or digital calendars to allocate specific time slots for each task. Consistency in your routine can reduce the urge to procrastinate.

Mindfulness

Mindfulness and self-awareness are valuable tools. Practicing mindfulness helps you become more aware of when and why you are procrastinating. This awareness allows you to address the underlying emotions or thoughts driving the behavior. Techniques such as meditation or deep breathing exercises can reduce anxiety, making it easier to start tasks.

Reward yourself

Reward yourself for completing tasks. Positive reinforcement can be a strong motivator. Whether it's taking a break, enjoying a treat, or engaging in a favorite activity, rewarding yourself can create a positive association with completing tasks. Over time, this can help in reducing procrastination.

Accountability

Lastly, accountability can make a significant difference. Sharing your goals with a colleague, friend, or mentor can create a sense of responsibility. Knowing that someone else is aware of your tasks and deadlines can push you to act. Consider joining a group or partnership where you can regularly check in on each other's progress.

Overcoming procrastination is a journey that requires persistence and self-compassion. It's important to acknowledge your progress, no matter how small, and not be too hard on yourself when setbacks occur.

Remember, the goal is not perfection but progress. With dedication and the right strategies, you can break the cycle of procrastination and take control of your time and productivity. Keep pushing forward—you've got this!

Case study: Henry's journey to overcome procrastination

Henry, a highly qualified and competent vehicle mechanic, had spent the better part of his career working at a prominent dealership. He enjoyed the hands-on nature of his job, where he excelled at diagnosing and fixing complex mechanical issues. His dedication and skill did not go unnoticed, leading to a well-earned promotion to workshop manager. However, this new role came with unexpected challenges that Henry had not expected.

Suddenly, Henry found himself overwhelmed by tasks that were far removed from his comfort zone. The job now involved a significant amount of administration, human resources management, planning, and report writing. These were not areas where Henry felt confident, and soon, procrastination began to set in.

At first, he would delay tasks that felt unfamiliar or uncomfortable, rationalizing that they could wait until later. But as the days turned into weeks, these tasks piled up, creating a growing sense of dread and anxiety.

Henry's procrastination began to have noticeable effects. Reports were submitted late, planning sessions were rushed, and the overall efficiency of the workshop started to decline. Despite his best efforts, Henry couldn't seem to break free from the cycle. The more he delayed, the more daunting the tasks became, which only reinforced his procrastination.

Fortunately, Henry had a caring friend named Greg, who noticed the changes in Henry's behavior. Greg had been through similar struggles in his own career and recognized the signs of procrastination and overwhelm. Rather than confronting Henry directly, Greg approached the situation with empathy. Over coffee one day, Greg gently brought up the topic of how challenging the new role must be. Henry, relieved to share his struggles, opened up about his difficulties.

Greg suggested several techniques that had helped him in the past. He introduced Henry to the **Pomodoro Technique**, explaining how it could break tasks into smaller, more manageable chunks. By focusing for just 25 minutes at a time, Henry found that even the most daunting tasks were easier to start. The short breaks allowed him to reset, preventing burnout and keeping his focus throughout the day.

Greg also recommended that Henry start **goal setting**. Together, they broke down Henry's weekly tasks into daily goals, focusing on one thing at a time. This approach helped Henry feel a sense of accomplishment at the end of each day, rather than being overwhelmed by everything he had to do.

However, the journey was not without setbacks. There were days when old habits crept back in, and Henry found himself slipping into procrastination again. The pressure of the role sometimes triggered his anxiety, leading him to avoid certain tasks. But Greg encouraged him to stay the course, reminding him that progress wasn't always linear. They discussed how **mindfulness and self-awareness** could help Henry recognize when he was procrastinating and why. By acknowledging his feelings without judgment, Henry gradually learned to manage them more effectively.

Over the course of several months, Henry noticed significant improvements. The workshop's efficiency started to recover, and Henry found himself enjoying the managerial aspects of his role more.

He realized that while the tasks were different from what he was used to, they also offered new challenges that he could grow into. The confidence he gained from overcoming procrastination allowed him to fully embrace his new responsibilities.

Today, Henry continues to apply the techniques Greg introduced, using them to stay on top of his work. While he still faces challenges, he no longer feels overwhelmed by them. Instead, he approaches each day with a clear plan and the knowledge that he can manage whatever comes his way.

Henry's story is a testament to the power of persistence, the importance of support, and the impact that overcoming procrastination can have on both personal and professional growth.

——◄O►——

Section recap

In this section, we explored the complexities of procrastination and its impact on both personal and professional life. Understanding procrastination is the first step in overcoming it, as it allows us to address the root causes rather than just the symptoms.

We discussed practical strategies, such as the Pomodoro Technique, goal setting, and mindfulness, which can help break the cycle of procrastination. These techniques, while challenging to implement consistently, can lead to significant improvements in productivity and well-being.

The case study of Henry illustrated how procrastination can manifest even in skilled professionals and how support and persistence can lead to overcoming it. By applying these strategies and staying mindful of potential setbacks, you can take control of your time and work more effectively.

——◄O►——

The building blocks of time management for improved productivity

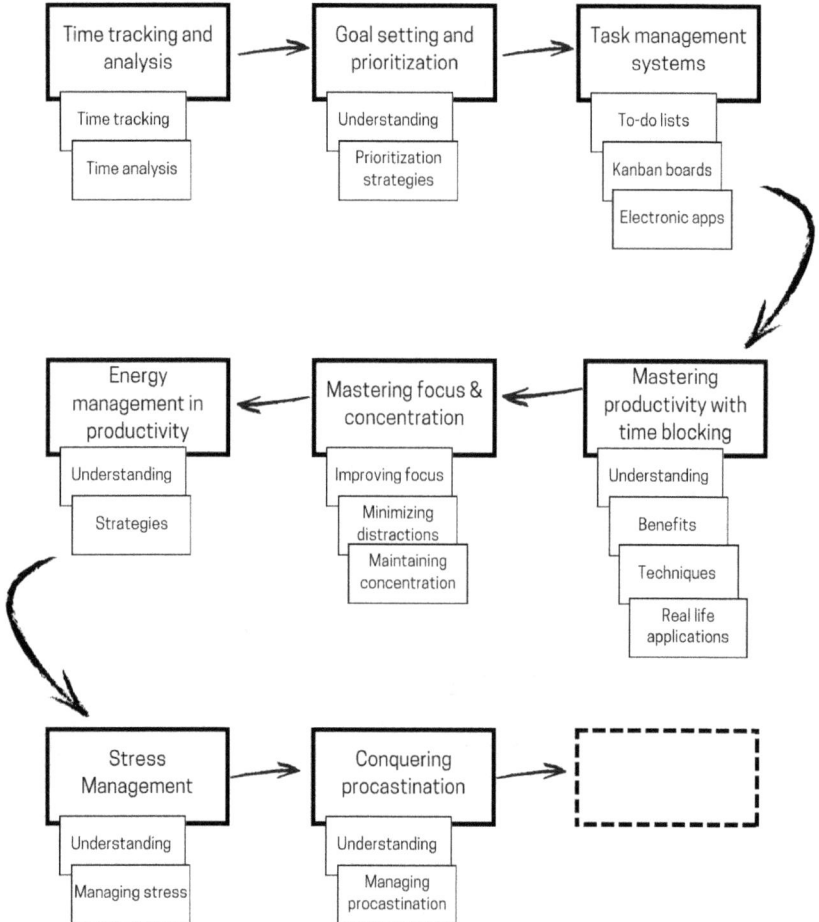

```
┌─────────────────┐     ┌─────────────────┐     ┌─────────────────┐
│ Time tracking and│ ──▶ │ Goal setting and │ ──▶ │ Task management  │
│     analysis     │     │  prioritization  │     │     systems      │
└─────────────────┘     └─────────────────┘     └─────────────────┘
  │ Time tracking │       │ Understanding │       │ To-do lists │
  │ Time analysis │       │ Prioritization│       │ Kanban boards │
                          │  strategies   │       │ Electronic apps │
```

- Time tracking and analysis
  - Time tracking
  - Time analysis
- Goal setting and prioritization
  - Understanding
  - Prioritization strategies
- Task management systems
  - To-do lists
  - Kanban boards
  - Electronic apps
- Energy management in productivity
  - Understanding
  - Strategies
- Mastering focus & concentration
  - Improving focus
  - Minimizing distractions
  - Maintaining concentration
- Mastering productivity with time blocking
  - Understanding
  - Benefits
  - Techniques
  - Real life applications
- Stress Management
  - Understanding
  - Managing stress
- Conquering procastination
  - Understanding
  - Managing procastination

Action plan

To put this section into action, you can do the following

- List the eight techniques to overcome procrastination.

- Decide which technique(s) to implement right away.

- Plan and diarize those techniques you decide to implement at a later stage.

Chapter 9
Conclusion

"Inaction breeds doubt and fear. Action breeds confidence and courage. If you want to conquer fear, do not sit home and think about it. Go out and get busy."

Dale Carnegie

Recap of key topics

Throughout this book, we have delved into essential strategies and techniques to master productivity, manage time, and enhance overall efficiency in both personal and professional settings.

Here's a recap of the key topics covered in Sections 1 through 9.

The **Introduction** set the stage by emphasizing the importance of time management in entrepreneurship. We explored how effectively managing time can lead to increased productivity and profitability, while also maintaining a healthy work-life balance.

In **Section 1**, we discussed the critical role of **time tracking and analysis**. This section highlighted the need to monitor how time is spent daily, using tools and techniques to identify inefficiencies and improve productivity. Understanding where your time goes allows you to make informed decisions that align with your goals.

Section 2 focused on **effective goal setting and prioritization**. Here, we learned about setting clear, actionable goals and prioritizing tasks that have the most significant impact on those goals. The strategies provided in this section help ensure that your efforts are always aligned with your highest objectives.

Section 3 introduced various **task management systems**. This section covered tools and methodologies that help you organize and manage tasks efficiently. From simple to-do lists to advanced project management software, these systems are designed to streamline your workflow and keep you on track.

In **Section 4**, we explored the power of **time blocking** as a productivity tool. This technique involves dedicating specific blocks of time to tasks, minimizing distractions, and improving focus. Time blocking is essential for managing your day effectively and ensuring that critical tasks receive the attention they deserve.

Section 5 delved into **mastering focus and concentration**. We discussed techniques for enhancing your ability to concentrate on tasks, such as minimizing distractions, practicing mindfulness, and limiting multitasking. Mastering these skills is crucial for achieving deep work and keeping elevated levels of productivity.

Section 6 was dedicated to **energy management**. This section emphasized the importance of aligning tasks with your natural energy levels to maximize output and efficiency. By understanding and managing your energy, you can achieve more without exhausting yourself, leading to sustainable productivity.

Section 7 addressed **thriving under pressure through stress management**. We explored strategies for managing stress, such as mindfulness, exercise, and time management, to maintain mental and emotional well-being while staying productive under pressure.

Finally, **Section 8** tackled the challenge of **conquering procrastination**. We explored the root causes of procrastination and provided actionable strategies to overcome it, ensuring that you stay on track and achieve your goals without unnecessary delays.

Each of these sections has equipped you with practical tools and insights to manage your time, energy, and focus effectively. By applying these strategies, you can enhance your productivity, reduce stress, and achieve your personal and professional goals more efficiently.

Concluding thoughts

As you close this book, remember that productivity and effective time management are not isolated skills; they are interconnected facets of a successful life and business.

Each strategy, technique, and tool we've discussed is part of a larger puzzle. When you improve in one area, you often see benefits in others, sometimes without even realizing it.

For instance, mastering focus naturally enhances your ability to avoid procrastination. Likewise, understanding how to manage your energy not only boosts productivity but also reduces stress. These elements work together, creating a synergy that elevates your overall effectiveness. The journey to mastering these skills is continuous, and it's okay to take it one step at a time.

Remember, the goal isn't perfection but progress. Each small improvement you make contributes to a more balanced, fulfilling life. Embrace the process, be patient with yourself, and celebrate each victory, no matter how small. By applying what you've learned, you're not just becoming more productive—you're building a foundation for sustained success and well-being.

You have the tools and knowledge to take control of your time, energy, and focus. Now, it's up to you to put them into practice. Keep striving, stay inspired, and remember that every step forward is a step toward your goals.

The building blocks of time management for improved productivity

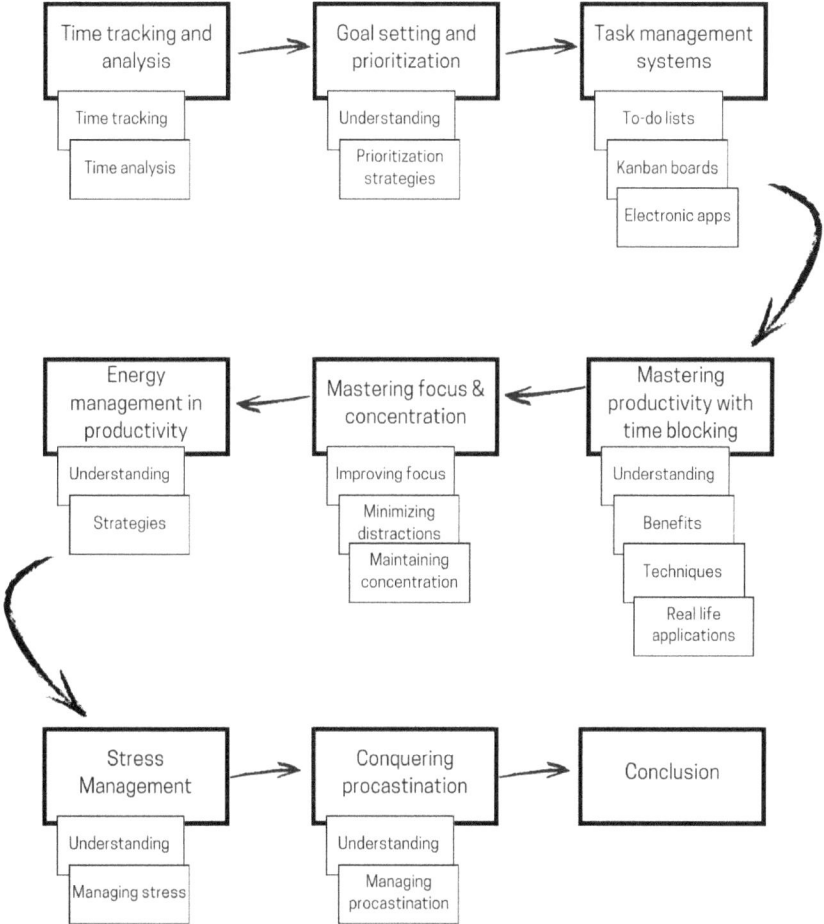

Time tracking and analysis	Goal setting and prioritization	Task management systems
Time tracking	Understanding	To-do lists
Time analysis	Prioritization strategies	Kanban boards
		Electronic apps

Energy management in productivity	Mastering focus & concentration	Mastering productivity with time blocking
Understanding	Improving focus	Understanding
Strategies	Minimizing distractions	Benefits
	Maintaining concentration	Techniques
		Real life applications

Stress Management	Conquering procastination	Conclusion
Understanding	Understanding	
Managing stress	Managing procastination	

Next steps

You've reached the end of this book, but your journey toward mastering productivity and time management is just beginning. The strategies and tools you've learned are powerful, but their true value lies in putting them into practice. The next step is to act.

Start by reviewing the key points and strategies that resonated most with you. Focus on implementing one or two changes at a time. Small, consistent steps often lead to the most noteworthy progress. Don't feel pressured to apply everything at once; gradual implementation will yield more sustainable results.

Appendix A is your guide as you move forward. It has a master action plan—a summary of all the Sections' action plans. Use it as a roadmap to prioritize your actions and track your progress. This plan will help you stay organized and ensure that you're applying the lessons from each section effectively.

Remember, **Appendix B** has more resources to support your journey. It includes a free Excel download and various links to YouTube videos. These tools are designed to reinforce the strategies discussed in this book and help you stay on course.

Take these next steps with confidence. You have the knowledge and tools to transform how you manage your time and energy. By applying these strategies, you're setting yourself up for lasting success. Keep pushing forward and remember that every small step you take brings you closer to achieving your goals.

Thank you for reading!

If you found this book helpful, I'd greatly appreciate it if you could take a moment to leave a review on Amazon. Your feedback not only helps me improve but also assists other readers in finding the right resources. Scan the QR code (or click on it) to share your thoughts.

I appreciate your support!

Appendix A: Action plan

Combining the various sections' plans, you can use this plan to help you plot your way.

Time tracking and analyses

1. Track Time: Choose a tool or method that fits your needs (e.g., Toggl, journal).

2. Analyze Data: Review daily and weekly reports to identify patterns and trends.

3. Identify Time Wasters: Spot inefficiencies and avoid unnecessary tasks.

4. Improve Schedule: Align high-impact tasks with your productivity peaks.

5. Experiment and Adjust: Try different strategies like time-blocking and delegation.

Goals and priorities

Commit to Writing:

1. Document your goals, tasks, and priorities in a journal,

planner, or digital tool.

Identify Big-Picture Goals:

1. Clearly define your overarching goals (career, personal development, health, or business).

2. Ensure each goal is Specific, Measurable, Achievable, Relevant, and Time-bound (SMART).

Break Down Goals into Actionable Tasks:

1. Divide each big-picture goal into smaller, manageable tasks.

2. Assign target dates for completing each task.

Prioritize Daily:

1. Begin each day or week by reviewing your goals and identifying top-priority tasks.

2. Use the ABCDE method or Eisenhower Matrix to rank tasks based on importance and urgency.

3. Focus on completing A-tasks (most important) first.

Time Block High-Value Activities:

1. Allocate specific blocks of time in your schedule for high-priority tasks.

2. Ensure these blocks are free from distractions.

Review and Adjust:

1. Regularly assess your progress toward your goals.

2. Adjust your tasks, priorities, and timelines as needed.

3. Stay flexible and adapt to changes in circumstances.

Visualize Success:

1. Spend a few minutes each day visualizing the completion of your top-priority tasks.

2. Imagine the positive outcomes and feelings associated with achieving your goals.

Track Progress and Celebrate Milestones:

1. Monitor your progress toward each goal.

2. Celebrate when you reach key milestones to keep motivated!

Task management systems

1. Consider your requirements

2. Choose the task management system that aligns with your requirements.

Time blocking

1. Follow the steps discussed in "Understanding time blocking".

2. Study the suggested time-blocking techniques and choose which one(s) to apply.

Focus and concentration

Decide which strategies or techniques to use for each of the following:

1. To improve focus.

2. To minimize distractions.

3. To improve concentration.

Strategies for maximizing productivity with energy management

1. List the seven strategies for maximizing productivity with energy management.

2. Apply these strategies in chronological order.

Coping strategies for stress management

1. List the seven coping strategies for managing stress.

2. Decide which strategy to start with right away, and which ones to add later.

Overcoming procrastination

1. List the eight techniques to overcome procrastination.

2. Decide which technique(s) to implement right away.

3. Plan and diarize those techniques you decide to implement at a later stage.

Appendix B: Resources

Eisenhower matrix

Beginner's Guide

This YouTube video does well to explain the use of the matrix: https://www.youtube.com/watch?v=tLLyi50M5KM

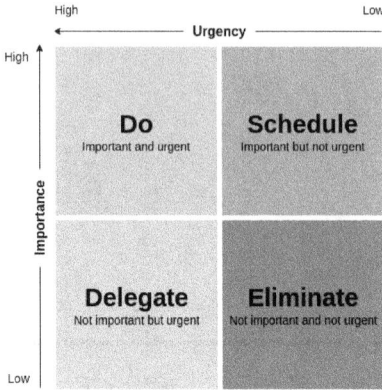

Kanban boards

How to use a physical board

This YouTube video will help you implement a basic yet effective physical Kanban board:
https://www.youtube.com/watch?v=7MDWfAsrrtw

Excel spreadsheet with Kanban board

We have created a very versatile Kanban board in Excel for you to start with. It is easy to use and includes instructions. Follow the download instructions at the beginning of this Appendix.

Custom build your own Karban board in Excel

This YouTube video is long and detailed, but for those of you who need a more elaborate Kanban board with loads of functionality, this is worth a watch:
https://www.youtube.com/watch?app=desktop&v=3qbU5S8ZaEA

Illustration of the Pomodoro technique

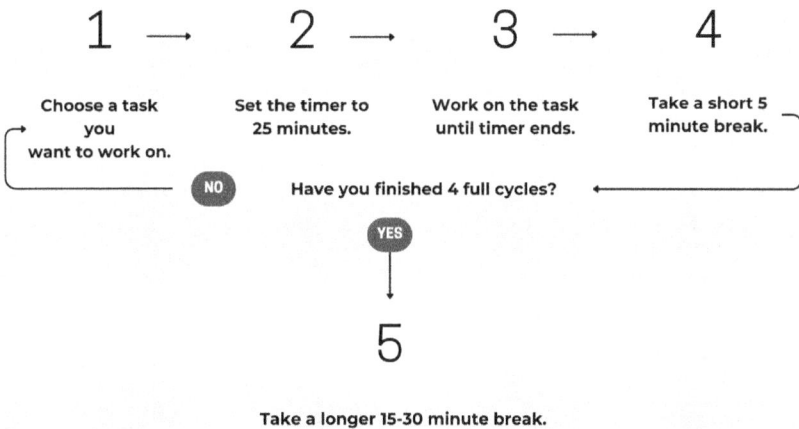

1 → 2 → 3 → 4

Choose a task you want to work on.

Set the timer to 25 minutes.

Work on the task until timer ends.

Take a short 5 minute break.

NO   **Have you finished 4 full cycles?**

YES

5

Take a longer 15-30 minute break.

About the Author

Ellen Sedge is a seasoned entrepreneur with a career that has evolved from mastering financial systems to helping other entrepreneurs. With a background that spans from simple bookkeeping to advanced financial systems, Ellen founded a training academy early in her career and later served as an independent consultant for medium-sized businesses.

Seeking a better work-life balance, she transitioned to a home-based business, selling personal care products, and later launched two other businesses in another country. As an avid reader and keen traveler, Ellen has visited countries on five continents, enriching her perspective.

Her firsthand experience in time management and discipline gained from working independently provides valuable insights to entrepreneurs in the small business sector and digital nomads alike. Ellen's passion lies in empowering others to navigate the challenges of entrepreneurship with confidence and skill.

About the Publisher

Impisi™ Media is a dynamic publishing company dedicated to creating and distributing high-quality intellectual property, including books, e-books, audiobooks, and journals.

Our content is crafted to inform, inspire, and empower a global audience. Our commitment to innovation and excellence drives us to deliver content that resonates and adds value to our readers and listeners.

Visit our website https://impisimedia.com

f facebook.com/impisimedia

○ instagram.com/impisimedia

𝓟 pinterest.com/impisimedia

www.ingramcontent.com/pod-product-compliance
Lightning Source LLC
LaVergne TN
LVHW051349080426
835509LV00020BA/3363